DYING and GRIEVING

Opening to

DYING and GRIEVING

A Sacred Journey

Ron Valle and Mary Mohs

YES
INTERNATIONAL
PUBLISHERS

SAINT PAUL, MINNESOTA

For information and permission address:

Yes International Publishers
1317 Summit Avenue
Saint Paul, MN 55105-2602
651-645-6808
www.yespublishers.com
yes@yespublishers.com

Library of Congress Cataloging-in-Publication Date

Valle, Ronald S.
  Opening to dying and grieving : a sacred journey / Ron Valle and Mary Mohs.
    p. cm.
  Includes bibliographical references.
  ISBN-13 : 978-0-936663-40-1
  1. Death—Religious aspects.   2. Bereavement—Religious aspects.
  3. Grief—Religious aspects   4. Suffering—Religious aspects.
  5. Termona I. Mohs, Mary E. II. Title.
    BL504.V35 2006
    155.9'37—dc22   2006024021

Cover art "Two Egrets" by Roderick MacIver of *Heron Dance*
Interior crane drawing by Kate Poole

To the memory of my loving parents, Elso and Mabel – RV

*To my loved ones who no longer live in this world: my son, Teddy,
my brother, Jimmy, my parents, Marie and Walter,
and my grandparents, Josephine and Jerome – MM*

*To all of the dying and grieving clients
who have opened their hearts to us,
thereby helping us to better understand
the nature of
living, dying, and grieving.*

Acknowledgements

I wish to express my deepest gratitude for the love, inner strength, and commitment of my dear wife, Valerie. Her unselfish efforts to support me while attempting to understand my spiritual journey has made my contribution to this book possible. I am grateful for the steady encouragement of our now adult children, Demian, Alexa, and Chris. My family is a true blessing in my life. I wish to acknowledge the gentle yet powerful influence that my friend and colleague, Rolf von Eckartsberg, has had on how I see the world, myself, and others. In both his life and death, Rolf taught me so much regarding what lies beyond the linear causal way of "being-in-the-world." Regarding our shared commitment to being with the dying and grieving, I offer my heartfelt appreciation for my friend and co-author, Mary Mohs, whose unwavering faith and devotion to her spiritual life has been, and continues to be, a steady and reliable source of inspiration. I am grateful for all that I have learned about the relationship between grieving and the sacred realms by observing how she copes with the many personal losses in her life. — RV

I would like to express my deepest appreciation to my husband, Greg, who has been instrumental in his support of my work and who walked the path of sorrow and love with me following our son Ted's death. I also want to acknowledge our three children, Jacquie, Deborah, and Greg, together with their families, for their love and inspiration, and my two living brothers, Martin and Robert, for their guidance and spiritual sensitivity over the years. There are many friends and relatives that have encouraged me on my journey. I offer special thanks to my longtime friends, Rebecca Grado and Jill LeBeau, for their support and encouragement in writing this book. I would especially like to thank Ron Valle for his masterful skill in understanding and articulating my deepest feelings when I could not find the words to express them. His wisdom and friendship have greatly enhanced my journey in the years that I have known him. I will always be grateful for the spiritual knowledge that we have gained in writing this book. — MM

We offer our sincere gratitude to Theresa King and Swami Jaidev Bharati for their personal support over the years, and for recognizing the value and potential of this book. We offer a special thank you to Theresa at Yes International Publishers for her careful and skillful editing of our writing. Our thanks also go out to the friends and colleagues who offered valuable insights, feedback, and commentary after reading the manuscript in its evolving forms. They include Valerie, Greg, Jacqueline Mohs, M.D., Bis Kruger, Swami Veda Bharati, Rt. Rev. William Swing, William Lamers, M.D., Terri O'Fallon, Sister Rebecca Shinas, Tina Amorok, Thomas Forest, Richard Valinsky, Jeanne Martel, and Diane Thorson.

With humility and respect, we honor our spiritual teachers. Their guidance and grace continue to bring light to the dark places in our minds and hearts.

Contents

Foreword

With unassailable assurance, the instinct for self-preservation looms through all walks of life. Behind that conviction, like an ever-present shadow, lies a dread reality that few want to discuss, much less confront. As Homer remarks in the *Odyssey*, "It is our common lot to die, and the gods themselves cannot rescue even one they love when death, that stretches all men out, lays its dread hand upon him."

That challenge is taken up by Ron Valle and Mary Mohs. In both a forthright manner, and an evident breadth of balanced sympathy, these authors gradually walk the reader through the labyrinth of the inevitable—living, dying, and grieving. Borrowing insight from those acute writers who have preceded them, and with the added experience of their background in yoga philosophy, they circumspectly illuminate the human confrontation with a seemingly implacable foe.

The authors' hopeful exposition, enthralling as well as controversial, refuses to back away from the emotional issues associated with the never-ending, tearful sorrow that can haunt our days. While Aeschylus pronounces in his *Niobe,*

> Alone of gods, Death has no love for gifts,
> Libation helps you not, nor sacrifice.
> He has no altar, and hears no hymns;
> From him alone Persuasion stands apart.

Our authors uniquely offer to those innocently caught up in an almost unendurable episode of life and death both a humane solace and a transcendental resolution. Death may claim the skirmish with our bodies, but, as our perceptive authors remind us, our spirit always triumphs in the final campaign. After pondering the thoughts and experiences in these pages, the reader will sing with Saint Paul, "O death, where is thy victory? O death, where is thy sting?"

Swami Jaidev Bharati

(formerly Justin O'Brien, Ph.D.)
Institute of the Himalayan Tradition
Saint Paul, Minnesota, February, 2006

Preface

Delete Death![1]

We fail to erase "death" from our writings of our fate; we fail to delete it from the programs in our minds. The undying myth called death revives itself, raises its fearsome hood, as though a reality, each time a creature makes the (re-)appearance called birth.

Each time the Master Alchemist prepares plans to alter our wrinkles into the freshness of a new infant's smooth skin, we cry out, "Death!" Each time the Master Builder seeks to demolish an old decrepit chamber and make for us a new one with better amenities, we shout out, "Death!"

The theologians debate about the best means to kill the elephant who is not in the room, nor in the forest. They sharpen their word-darts, wishing somehow to be able to shoot them at the no-elephant so it would not pick us up with its only-in-myth-hanging long trunk and trample us with the shadow feet of fear. Sages and masters, prophets and saints, for a thousand generations, have sung to us the songs of our immortality, but we won't listen, so enamoured are we of our favorite myth, the myth of death.

In the *Katha Upanishad*, Nachiketa demolished it. Bhishma asked, "What can death do to us (*kim no mrtuh karishyati*)?"[2]

The sage Sanatsujata of the *Mahabharata*, blessed to remain a child perennially, stated categorically, "There is no such thing as death (*na mrtyur asti*)."[3]

The Vedas, Upanishads, the Bible, other scriptures, Lao Tsu, and Socrates all showed us the key to press to delete the program called death from our minds. But we just refuse, and still run around in panic, crying and shouting all over the city streets, "The sky is falling. Death! Death! Death is on its way!"

Everyone prays, "May I not die," but the Vedic sage prays:

May I not, O Lord of Universal Law,
Re-enter this house of clay.
(*Mo shu varuna mrnmayam*
Graham rajann aham gamam)

And, when the Buddha opened his eyes upon reaching enlightenment, what were the first words that he uttered?

"I have seen you, O house-builder.
You shall build me no more a house!"

My own master, Swami Rama, before demolishing his old house so that he may live only in a house whose building blocks are Light, has tried to delete death from our minds in his book *Sacred Journey,* but, reading, we read it not.

May this book, herewith presented, help many to de-program the concept of the myth of death from their minds. May the *non-natus,* ever unborn (*a-janma*), non-geriatric, un-decaying, unwrinkled, never aging (*a-jara*), non-mortal, never dying (*a-mrtyu*),[4] in them come out yelling now, whispering then, silent again, "Here I am! Know me as it is I who is you, eternally immortal." Death, that was not, never was, an entity, remains banished to be so. It was ever a *vikalpa,* a verbal fantasy without an object.[5]

Ron Valle and Mary Mohs, both longtime meditators, have chosen to share this wealth and give a selfless service to aid in every seeker's contemplations. With all blessings that the re-cognition (*praty-abhi-jna*) of our non-mortality confers.

Swami Veda Bharati
(formerly Usharbudh Arya, Ph.D.)
Swami Rama Sadhaka Grama
Rishikesh, India, August, 2005

Introduction

Life presents us with many opportunities to experience both pleasure and pain. When we see the beauty and mystery in the world around us, we often feel joy and our hearts naturally open. If, however, we hold on too tightly when the kaleidoscope of life changes, we suffer. This book examines the nature of attachment and how the tendency of the mind to cling to people, places, and things can be brought into the light of awareness, thereby easing our suffering. Bringing our awareness to the times of grieving and dying can be especially powerful as opportunities on the spiritual journey.

We are Mary Mohs and Ron Valle. Together we represent Awakening: A Center for Exploring Living and Dying. Through the years, we have found that our spiritual paths have involved learning how to let go of our attachments so that we can love more deeply and accept the challenges of life. We have also learned that the pain resulting from the loss of our attachments can be useful in learning how to simply be with life, and seeing the essence that lies beyond this mundane world and unites us all. We would like to give you an overview of our lives, our organization, and the development of this book.

I, Mary, first encountered death at the age of twelve when my grandmother died. The world suddenly became a different place since my grandmother had been like a mother to me. In my twenties, when my children were still quite young, I again realized how quickly my life could change when my father died of cancer and my brother died in a motorcycle accident, both within a year's time. These experiences led me to work as a nurse at a Veterans Administrative Hospital. Having seen so many veterans using alcohol and other drugs as a way of attempting to cope with life and their pain, I became a substance abuse counselor.

When my son tragically died in an accident in 1985, I decided then and there to begin using my experience of intense grief as a conscious spiritual practice. My spiritual journey intensified when I attended graduate school, earning my master's degree in transpersonal counseling psychology, and then found myself volunteering to be with those facing a life-threatening illness and their families. My opening to dying and grieving continued after my mother was struck and killed by a car in January of 1997.

The major transformative experiences that I, Ron, have had began in July of 1975 with a near-fatal motorcycle accident that involved a near-death experience, three months in a body cast, a severe concussion, an extended loss of short-term memory, six surgeries in six months, and learning to read, speak, and walk again. I had been serving as a professor of psychology at the time of the accident.

In the following two years, my oldest son was born, my father-in-law died of cancer, and my mother, after being depressed for many years, took her own life. At this point, my interest in academic psychology and research became secondary to my desire to work as a clinician, helping individuals with chronic pain and stress-related disorders. I became a practicing psychologist in 1978 and founded the outpatient clinic of a university pain control center. My daughter and second son were born during the next four years, followed by my wife's brain surgery in September of 1982. Her post-surgical seizures have been part of our lives since that time. In the early 1980s, I began my volunteer work with those dying and grieving. After my stepmother's death in 1999, I took care of my aging father who was suffering from congestive heart failure and advanced diabetes. My father died in January of 2004.

Awakening: A Center for Exploring Living and Dying is a nonprofit organization that we founded in November of 1992. Starting this organization was a natural next step that followed our many years of service as volunteers with those coping with a life-threatening diagnosis. Awakening's mission statement is to encourage and support those who seek the direct personal experience of the sacred within. In this context, the times of dying and grieving are seen as spiritually auspicious times to awaken to our deeper essence or spiritual self.

This book is about the inseparability of living, dying, and grieving. Speaking of any one of them includes, by its very nature, the other two. In our worldly existence, life and death are defined in terms of each other, while change and loss are part of life's tapestry. Our response to that loss, our grief, seems unavoidable since we become emotionally attached to special people and things in our lives. Death and dying are ultimately about life and living. Unfortunately, many of us wait until the end of our lives to truly open to life and find the authenticity that is necessary to truly live life to the fullest.

This book is not a book on the why or what of death and grief, but, rather, on the how—namely, how to be with and use the pain of loss in order to gain a deeper understanding of what lies beyond this mundane realm of reality. This new understanding then serves as a key to discovering the sacred treasure that lies within.

While the spiritual principles presented in this book are drawn primarily from our knowledge of yoga philosophy and psychology, we regard these principles as reflecting an underlying and universal truth. They are, therefore, presented throughout the book through the eyes of many different authors who represent different religious and spiritual traditions.

The insights that we offer in this book regarding living, dying, and grieving come from our experience. Theories and other intellectual understandings are important in that they help orient and quiet the thinking mind. The lessons learned from personal experience, however, are the most lasting—they rest in our hearts. We offer our experience to you, and invite you to open fully to the dying and grieving in your life, both that of others as well as your own. Your own experience will then guide you in realizing what is true for you, and what is not, when hearing the words of others.

Only when we face our grief and pain, and move through it, can we find the essence of the true life within us that remains unaffected by the changing world. The divine reality that lies outside of space and time was never born, and, therefore, never dies. Only our direct personal experience of this divine realm can validate this reality. We hope that our writing is helpful to you in your attempts to realize the sacred within. We conclude this introduction and open this book with the reflections of Arjuna Ardagh:

> Radical awakening is the moment when you taste reality outside the limiting confines of the mind, when you know yourself to be much bigger than—yet still containing—the body, beyond birth and death, eternally free.[1]

Mary Mohs and Ron Valle
Brentwood, California
August, 2006

Chapter 1
Living, Dying, and Grieving

While God was creating the universe, He called upon an angel, telling the angel that He had one last job to do. The angel was to help God hide the most precious gift—lasting peace and joy. This is the treasure of life. "Because this treasure is valuable beyond description I want you to hide it so that humans will know its value to be immeasurable when it's found." So the angel thought of several hiding places: the highest mountain, the great desert wilderness, the vast reaches of the universe. But God was not satisfied. All of these felt like places where the treasure would be too easily found. Finally, with a flash of inspiration, the Creator said: "Hide the treasure of life within the human being. He will look there last and, when he finally finds it, he will know how precious this treasure truly is."

Swami Rama of the Himalayas[1]
Sacred Journey

We know in our hearts that living and dying are inseparable, each dependent on the other for its sense and purpose. They are so inextricably intertwined that in our day-to-day understanding and language one actually has no meaning without the other. They are quite literally two sides of the same coin, not just in a philosophical sense, but in an actual lived-sense as well.

If, for example, one would like to know how afraid one will be when receiving one's terminal diagnosis, one only has to look at how afraid one is to live fully right now. To live fully is to love without fear, to give of oneself without any condition or expectation of something in return. From this perspective, fear of death and fear of life are truly one and the same.

Life and death are everywhere, whether it be the birth of a new idea or a leaf falling from a tree. Dying refers to the most profound experience in life. The fact and mystery of death is with us every moment of every day; it lies in the very fabric of our lives. The inevitability of our own impending death reminds us that life is limited, yet, when we live with this awareness, every moment of our lives becomes that much more precious. Being mindful of death thereby enhances life.

Life involves constant change. Everything is born, everything changes, everything dies. All things begin and all things end. To the extent that we base our happiness on the condition that someone or something will not change or die mirrors the degree of grief that we will experience when that person or thing does eventually change or is suddenly gone.

Grieving is, thus, a part of living. We die into the way things are when we grieve, and we grieve the loss of everything we have in this world when we die. In opening to living, dying, and grieving, one cannot truly understand any one of these processes without both explicitly and implicitly addressing the other two.

Yet, we resist and fear this change that is so inherent in life. Theresa King addresses this very issue in *The Spiral Path*. "We fear change because we believe that externals control our lives. In order to feel safe, we need all of life's externals in place, remaining the same as they were, so we can cope with them. We do this even if we are unhappy with the result. Should we be offered a chance to change our situation to something new or unknown, we often choose to stay exactly where we are."[2] Of all the changes that occur in life, the single greatest change is marked by death, so that choosing "to stay exactly where we are" ultimately means wanting to remain alive just as we are.

FEAR OF DEATH

Traditionally, ways of being with grieving, dying, and suffering reflect, on an institutional level, the deepest individual fear—the fear of death. Rather than being recognized as the natural companion of life, death has been seen as an enemy to be conquered with our latest drugs and surgical techniques. Or, when it cannot be avoided or significantly delayed, it has been hidden away in nursing homes or the back rooms of special hospital floors.

The impact of this institutionalized fear and denial on the individual facing a life-threatening condition has been immense. Surrounded by those who have not examined their own feelings or faced their own fears, many have suffered and died alone without an opportunity to express their emotions or to share their experience with a compassionate, listening other. Literally tied to life-sustaining machines, many have died in an atmosphere ranging from cool, professional distance to an actual avoidance on both a physical and emotional level. This pervasive attitude has also affected issues related to death and dying, including the nature of grief and the grieving process,[3] and euthanasia and the right to die.[4]

All our fears have their origin in the fear of death. If we turn and face death for what it is and, thereby, come to peace with our mortality, all other fears dissolve, including the fear of pain and suffering. If one's mortality is accepted, not just intellectually, but in the core of one's being, what is there to be afraid of? Our neighbor's opinion of us? Our new car being scratched?

No one has ever been hurt by death. It is the fear of death that creates the suffering. If death is embraced as safe and natural, what can possibly harm us?

This same fear of death, left unexamined and unfelt, spills over into our everyday lives. From our desire to alleviate this largely unconscious fear, we attempt to control others and the environment in which we find ourselves. This need to control keeps us from living in a creative, loving, and meaningful way. Rather than celebrating the rich variety and beauty of human expression, we tend to mistrust our spontaneous and passionate responses that are manifestations of the intuitively inspired, creative energy within us. Our fear of death keeps us from being fully alive!

EVOLVING ATTITUDES TOWARD DEATH AND DYING

Although still the norm, this collective response to death and dying is undergoing a slow but steady change. Reflecting an increasing awareness to the more subtle dimensions of dying and grieving, a number of areas stand out as central in the evolution of our own culture's understanding of these processes.

The Hospice Movement

The first, more formal, sign of the change in this understanding has been the hospice movement that began in England in the 1950s and has now taken root here in the United States.[5] In an attempt to humanize the dying process by providing sensitive and sympathetic care for the terminally ill and their families, hospice advocates have designed and established special programs for the dying who wish to die peacefully at home or at a separate hospice facility.

Regardless of where death occurs, hospice care is intended to make the last weeks or months of our lives easier to bear and, ideally, free from pain and fear. Although there are many aspects to the movement, the main focus of hospice is to bring physical and emotional support into the dying process for all involved.

The Influence of Elisabeth Kubler-Ross

In harmony with this increased emotional awareness and support is the work of Elisabeth Kubler-Ross, M.D.[6] Her efforts have brought a deeper and more sensitive understanding to the nature and pattern of the dying person's experience, and have led directly to a more compassionate way of being with the dying.[7] With the publication of her ground-breaking book, *On Death and Dying*, in 1969, her insights have changed the way that we think and feel about the end of our lives.

More specifically, she was the first to systematically observe, identify, and categorize five psychological sets or stages that the terminally ill experience as they proceed through the dying process. These stages do not always appear in exactly the same order or a one-time-only manner. For instance, a person may go back-and-forth among several different stages in a short period of time. In this way, these stages may more accurately be thought of as five ways of being rather than stages *per se*. In any event, they do have a tendency to appear in the following order:

> Denial — The initial response is often an avoidance of or refusal
> to accept the fact that one is dying.
>
> Anger — Feelings of rage, envy, and resentment often arise as the
> denial begins to ease.

Bargaining — Attempts to enter into some sort of agreement that may postpone the inevitable may then appear for brief periods.

Depression — Denial, anger, and bargaining are gradually replaced with a great sense of sadness and loss.

Acceptance — A quiet expectation of the inevitable follows.

These stages, thus identified, have become a definitive map for those working with the dying. They represented a new level of awareness regarding the experience of the dying person for our culture.

Near-Death Experience

In this same arena of investigating experience in the dying process, Raymond Moody, M.D.[8] has described the nature of the near-death experience.[9] With his 1975 book, *Life After Life,* Moody stood out as a natural scientist who boldly explored the subtler issues related to dying, including the metaphysical implications of the dying person's experience. Individuals who have been declared clinically dead, but who in some way return to life and waking consciousness, describe this experience with remarkable consistency across different persons, cultures, and medical conditions.

The near-death experience often includes some or all of the following characteristics: a sense of the ineffable or indefinable, hearing another reporting one's death, feelings of peace and quiet, being in a dark tunnel, hearing specific noises, being out of one's body, meeting others who have previously died, encountering a being of light, reviewing one's life, reaching a border or limit, and coming back to one's body and life. In Raymond Moody's presentation of these descriptions, the reported evidence of trans-physical and trans-emotional ways of being offer more subtle dimensions of experiences related to the dying process.

Spiritual Aspects of Dying and Grieving

The evolution of our culture's secular understanding took a significant step with the explicit recognition of the spiritual dimensions of dying and grieving in the teachings of Ram Dass[10] and Stephen Levine.[11] Ram Dass' story began when, as Richard Alpert, Ph.D., Harvard University professor and psychologist, he traveled to India in order to study with spiritual teachers in that part of the world. Returning to America in the early 1970s as Ram Dass, he has taught the sacred philosophies and practices of the East to countless individuals of all ages and backgrounds since that time. With charm and humor, he has a special gift for translating esoteric spiritual principles into contemporary American idiom.

In a similar way, Stephen Levine has applied many of these same principles in his writings that have been described as both poetic and personally transforming. His book, *Who Dies? An Investigation of Conscious Living and Conscious Dying*, published initially in 1982, has become a classic with regard to increasing our society's awareness of spiritual issues related to living, dying, and grieving.

By emphasizing the essence in each of us that is unaffected by death, Stephen Levine and Ram Dass have played a significant role in addressing spiritual experience *per se* as an integral part of living, suffering, and dying in current American culture.[12] They speak, for example, of that which doesn't change behind all of the world's ever changing phenomena. Their contemporary presentation of spiritual tenets are wholly consistent with the teachings of many renowned spiritual figures representing the world's great spiritual traditions who have described the nature of who we are before we entered this body, how this essence is here, right now, even as the body-object itself is aging and changing, and the way in which this soul-essence will continue after death when identity with the body has ended and the body has decayed.

In the context of becoming aware of our spiritual essence, serving others selflessly in life[13] and surrendering one's self-identity as a unique body and ego in death are, in the end, two facets of the same process—spiritual awakening. Both entail a process of letting go of habitual ways of defining oneself and being with the fear of opening into the unknown, of realizing that one's nature extends beyond the self-imposed limits of the ego-self. It is here, in this process of self-transformation, that spiritual experience becomes the ground for understanding, not as a blind belief in something more important or greater than oneself, but as an actual experience, or felt presence, of a new way or mode of being.

The words one uses to describe these more subtle realms of experience are not particularly important here. In this context, there are many commonly used words to choose from, including spiritual, sacred, transcendent, soul, Self, essence, God, transpersonal, and divine. From the ancient philosophies that preceded yoga come terms such as *Brahman, atman, jiva,* and *purusha.* When all is literally said and done, however, what really matters is the immediate and direct experience of that to which all of these various words refer.

Seeing life and death as ultimately two facets of an ongoing spiritual journey or process offers a special opportunity for those who are knowingly approaching the end of their lives. From this perspective, dying and grieving become spiritually auspicious times to awaken to our essence or soul nature. In the midst of the ever-changing phenomenal world, dying and grieving offer a space or opening in one's life where personal priorities are rearranged, previously unconscious patterns are revealed, and deeper questions arise.

Important issues also arise for those working with the dying and grieving. It is often assumed, for example, that individuals who choose to be with those who are grieving and dying, experience sadness, fatigue, and depression much of the time. And, yes, those of us who spend a lot of time with the terminally ill and their loved ones have cried many tears. But the truth is that working in this arena brings one in direct contact with core issues within oneself over and over again. This process is often rich and fulfilling. The ego usually tends to run here and there chasing after promised pleasures, and it is especially fond of pushing away pain. If you push away death, however, you push away life, because death is part of life.

If, therefore, one stays present with the reality of dying, one's ego must turn and face its fears. There is no longer anywhere to hide. Avoiding pain no longer works as a protective strategy when one is reminded on a regular basis of one's deepest inner issues and what really matters in life. Rather than being the source of sadness and withdrawal, being with dying becomes a foundation for living life fully with more energy and greater awareness of self and others. Buddha advised his disciples to live with death on their shoulders. To the extent that you remember and live with the knowledge and awareness that your time here is very limited, that everything of this world without exception changes, how precious everyone and everything becomes.

These times represent true opportunities, for both the individual who is dying or grieving and for the one who chooses to be with this person, to become aware of that which doesn't change. These are, therefore, special times to ask those deeper questions regarding the nature of life and death in a spirit of mutual exploration. Who is it that lives and dies? What is the essence in each of us that is untouched by death? From where does grief arise? Is suffering inherent in loss? Is there a joy that goes deeper than our daily happiness and sadness, wellness and illness? What does healing really mean in the context of a life-threatening illness?[14]

By opening to such questions with a loving and peaceful presence, the person attending offers conscious and compassionate support for the one who is dying or grieving. Whenever there is suffering, there are opportunities for deepening the self-understanding and spiritual awareness of those involved. In this way, there is always grace in suffering. As the great yogi, Neem Karoli Baba, once said, "I love suffering. It brings me closer to God."

One might wonder what it would be like to live life, not only aware of life's losses and accepting of one's reactions to these losses, but also being aware of that which never changes, untarnished, unblemished, pure, outside of time and space. Our fear of pain and limited sense of self keep us, however, from sustaining this more balanced and open way of holding our experience.

Self-identity exists in many forms including reference to one's age, race, parents, intelligence, occupation, place of residence, and emotional state. The grossest level of self-identity, and perhaps the most powerful, is the identity with the physical body itself. If someone or something threatens to harm *your* body, an intense, instinctive, defensive reaction almost always follows, as if it were *you* that was being threatened.

This identity is so strong that it seems odd to even question its nature or limits. Swami Rama, in fact, sees our minds as addicted to their identification with the physical body, and that this primary addiction is the foundation of all our other addictive inclinations.[15] From this perspective, facing our mortality and opening to the fear of death leads us eventually to the realization that we are more than our bodies alone, and that death is just another change in the existential circumstance of the unchanging soul. As Swami Rama once said, death is a comma in the soul's journey, not a period at the end of life's sentence. When the core of our addictions and our deepest fear is faced, all of our other addictions and fears dissolve.

Without this deeper exploration and awareness of our soul identity, the sense that we are our bodies runs deep within us. "This is my body." "These are my arms." "This is my face." This belief is the primary reason why being with death and dying is so difficult for so many. Yet, this is also what makes working consciously with the dying process such an important opportunity regarding awareness of the sacred within, and, thereby, coming to realize that having a body is only one aspect of who we really are. Working with the dying and facing death is a primary forum for helping to question and, thereby, to dissolve this foundational level of personal bodily identification that keeps us from knowing our true nature as the immutable, eternal Self, from knowing that unchanging aspect of ourselves that never dies.

Have you ever been with someone who has died? In other words, have you ever been with a corpse, a cadaver, a dead body? If you have not, we highly recommend the experience, spiritually speaking, because it is here that no philosophical or mystical interpretations are needed to understand the clear, scientific, objective fact that the body is an object. In fact, science tells us that the cells that comprise the body are constantly regenerating, that there is this continuous process of death and birth such that, in cycles that span many years, every cell in the body is different. It literally becomes a different object, a different body, time and time again.

This seems initially puzzling since, even though we identify so directly and immediately with our bodies, we do not live as if we are a completely different person time and time again. We are aware that the body is like a puppet. It moves when we wish to move it—raise an arm, stand up, turn around—and lies still when we wish to be still. Opening to this puzzle, there appears to be a constant thread that spans the years of bodily aging and change—an awareness, a sense of "I" or "me" that both moves the body while, at the same time, is separate from what the body is or is not doing at any given moment.

When observed and investigated as an experience, this sense of "I" is a doorway into that which doesn't change, to that which lies beyond the physical realm of time, space, and causation, to that which is in the body, but not of it. Rajmani Tigunait in his book, *From Death To Birth*, notes that the body is like a rented apartment.[16] When the lease expires, we are evicted. This image raises still further questions: What is this body? What is its purpose? Whose body is this, really?

BRINGING AWARENESS TO DYING

When the person who is dying and the person who is attending this process agree to work together, a special type of relationship is formed. To the degree that spiritual awareness and compassion are the cornerstones of this living relationship, the dying process becomes a conscious dying for both involved. As an example of how this approach can manifest in the lives of two individuals who choose to bring awareness to the dying process, consider the text of this account describing Ron's relationship with a man in the latter stages of AIDS.

Michael is dying. He sees himself as a long-term survivor who has watched many of his closest friends die, one after the other, in the past few years. Of his twelve or so friends who tested HIV-positive years ago, only Michael and one other remain. He claims that he cannot go to another funeral or shed another tear. It's not that he doesn't care any longer, but that he's reached a core place within himself that is at peace with how it is. All of the old reasons that his mind would offer up about what he should do or how he should feel are simply gone. After so much loss and so much grief, his caring heart has been burned clean.

From these experiences and others, he knows AIDS well: what symptoms come along at what time, and what they mean regarding the quality of life and the closeness of death. He has been through pneumocystis twice, had his spleen surgically removed, and is now dealing with vomiting after almost every meal. He couldn't deny what's happening to him even if he wanted to. He tires very easily at this point, and wonders why he goes on.

I've been visiting with Michael for a few hours most every week. Sometimes we walk or run errands, most often we simply sit and talk, sketching out a spontaneous map of our experiences with each other, including those that touch his feelings about dying.

Last week he touched a deep and powerful place within himself as he described feeling the awesome inevitability of his approaching death. He has newly realized that there is nothing he can think or feel or do to avoid going through death's door, a passage he now faces with both human fear and an authentic, almost childlike excitement. As he shared his feelings, I felt as if he was whirling in a vortex, an experience of such sheer power and speed that it blurred my mind as I felt inexorably drawn into the mystery. He reflected on all of those many moments throughout his life when he thought he had a choice or an important decision to make, and how those same moments now appeared so illusory and quite irrelevant. I thought to myself, how liberating it is to feel freed from the demands of the deciding mind.

As Michael spoke, I crossed an edge inside of myself as I opened into the vortex with him. At that moment I became aware of, not only my own fear and excitement, but my unmistakable love for him. I felt our deep human connection as well as the simple fact that my own pain would be very real whenever it was that Michael died. It was here that I saw how much of my life and feeling I push away, how the vortex is always there to experience, yet how we all seem to live as if we were above it all, unaware of life's constant movement and constant change.

There is so much more to share: Michael's struggle with his ambivalence towards both life and death, his humor and joy at moments when the melodrama of life seems so absurd, his feelings about those close to him who need his support to help them cope with their feelings about his illness, and his incredible clarity and spiritual courage in opening to the process in which he finds himself. There are my own feelings of wonder and awe, wanting to help, spiritual presence, awkwardness, and just not knowing what to say or do much of the time, letting myself "be done" rather than doing; and how the vortex he described approaching death is so very similar to the vortex of love, the inevitable pull we all sense when we feel our hearts connect, the same pull we all believe we can resist by keeping our distance, defining boundaries, and keeping our hearts closed when the feeling of love gets too strong.

Our being with each other continued to be an incredible teaching until the time of Michael's death. It was only at that point that I could fully appreciate our shared exploration; how secrets of opening to life and death had slowly revealed themselves in whatever ways he and I had been ready and willing to hear.[17]

Chapter 2
The Process Of Dying

Since death, when we look closely, is [in the fabric] of our life, I have
formed so close an acquaintance with this truest and best friend of humankind
that its image no longer holds anything terrifying for me, but, rather, much
that is calming and consoling. And I thank my God for graciously granting me
the opportunity of learning that death is the key that unlocks for us the door of
true happiness.

Wolfgang Amadeus Mozart
April 4, 1787 letter on learning
that his father was dying

In our discussion of the spiritual aspects of dying and grieving in the previous chapter, the primary emphasis was on the formless, or that which doesn't change. Most of us, however, on a day-to-day, moment-to-moment basis, focus on the forms in our lives or, in other words, on that which changes.

It seems that in order to understand the deepest levels of living and dying, one must address and somehow integrate both the form, that all of us must eventually let go of, and the formless, that lies beyond the impermanency of this mundane world. To live with an open and balanced awareness of both the worldly and the transcendent realms is personally and spiritually challenging.

Christ addressed this distinction in John 8:23 when he said to the Pharisees, "You are of this world; I am not."[1]

Swami Rama has repeatedly advised those who seek to deepen their spiritual ground to "be in the world but not of it."

REVISITING THE STAGES

Elisabeth Kubler-Ross discussed in her book, *On Death and Dying,* her observations of over 200 individuals who were experiencing their last days on earth.[2] She found that, collectively, their experiences formed a general pattern represented by the five stages as mentioned earlier. Since the time of her original proposal, we have come to realize that these stages represent attempts to define particular processes in an otherwise dynamic flow of experience that unfolds at the time of dying. These stages are linear in that they tend to appear in the order Kubler-Ross initially proposed, but in their actual emergence throughout the dying process they often spiral, overlap, appear and disappear, come in waves, or return unpredictably, again and again, in a circular fashion.

From this more current perspective, we suggest that denial, anger, and bargaining (the first three stages) represent the resistance we experience in admitting to ourselves that we are dying. In the fourth stage, depression, we realize we are dying, but are yet unable to accept the truth of what is happening. Finally, in acceptance we no longer cling as we once did to people and things of the world, and realize that death is part of a greater reality. Here is the final episode of our lives, our last opportunity to see if we can truly open to "what is" and realize the inner treasure that is inherently ours. The dying process is truly the last part of our spiritual journey before we end our identification with earthly existence. Let's take a closer look at the experience of dying.

Denial

The first stage of this journey is denial. Often a person in denial will either try to push the illness out of his or her mind or constantly obsess about it. One may say, "The lab mixed up my files. There must be some mistake!" Others may become fixated on the surgery that revealed their terminal condition, or on the illness itself. At this point, they are unable to realize the impermanence of their lives. The following is an account of Mary's experience with the way in which denial can manifest.

A woman brought her nieces in for counseling with me when her sister, Kari, who was dying from a brain tumor, could no longer take care of them. Several weeks later, Kari came in with her sister and children. She walked very slowly towards my office. She was thin and frail and was wearing a bandana to hide the baldness caused by her chemotherapy treatments. During the session I asked Kari if there was anything she would like to say to the children about her illness, thinking that she would have some profound words to share with them before she died. She turned to the children and said, "I just want you to know that when I am well again, we will all take a trip to Disneyland." Her sister, who was very frustrated with her at this point, said to her, "Didn't you hear the doctor say four months ago that you only had about six more months to live?" Kari was shocked! It was as though she heard the fatal diagnosis for the first time.

So often we can see the denial of death in others, and have a difficult time understanding how they can be in denial when the reality is so obvious. When it is our turn to face death, how easy will it be for us to accept what is coming? It is not only when we are given the diagnosis of a terminal illness that we experience denial, but denial occurs throughout our lives. As we are aging, for instance, we find ways to avoid this fact. Cosmetics, hair dyes, tummy tucks, Botox® injections, and plastic surgery are just some of the ways we deny that our body is moving towards death. The attachment to our bodily form and its appearance is very strong.

Anger

In the anger stage we feel contracted, and everything in our lives feels wrong. Life simply isn't going the way we think it should. We feel powerless and want to feel a sense of control. Often the anger is directed towards the medical staff or our loved ones, and is seldom examined and opened to. Instead of responding with compassion, others often react and take the dying person's anger personally. This reaction, in turn, fuels the fire.

We all need to realize that lying beneath the dying person's anger are sadness, a terror of the unknown, and a burning desire to return to how it was before the illness came into their lives. True compassion comes when we allow the intensity of our anger to dissolve and focus on the more subtle feelings we may have within. Mary's experience with the transformation of anger is illustrated in the following story.

Many years ago when I was a nurse at a Veterans Administration hospital there was a man who was paraplegic and had recently been diagnosed with cancer. He was very obnoxious. He would throw things, spit at the nurses, and routinely curse and swear. Since every other nurse threatened to quit if they had to take care of him, I was usually the one who was assigned to him. I really didn't want to be around him, so I would do what I needed to do and leave his room as quickly as possible.

One day, he was so angry that he pulled himself up using the overhead bar and threw himself out of bed. I was stunned! I called for the doctor who, after examining him and putting him back into bed, scolded him for his behavior. The doctor then came out into the hall and commended me for being able to take care of such a man. As I was listening to these praises, I wondered what was wrong with this picture. Here I was able to enjoy life and do whatever I wished, while this man had no visitors, had alienated the nurses, and was unable to go anywhere. I decided I needed to change my attitude towards him.

That evening before going home, I read his chart from front to back. It was rich with the details of his life. He had been a very successful businessman, owned his own business, and had a family. One day, he had taken his family out for a drive. He had been drinking and, at a critical point, had misjudged the distance of an oncoming truck. An accident occurred and, as a result, his entire family was killed and he became paraplegic. He had also been transferred to the San Francisco area from southern California and had no friends who could visit with him.

The next morning, instead of seeing an angry patient that I had to take care of, I saw a human being in pain. Instead of doing what I needed to do and then leaving, I was able to listen to him from my heart. He didn't change immediately, but it didn't take long before he was able to shift his anger and feel heard and understood again. Within a few weeks, I was able to work with the hospital administration to enable him to return home. On the day he left, there were nurses and doctors from all over the hospital that came to say good-bye. I watched as tears streamed down his face. He had changed because someone had stopped reacting to his anger and, instead, had begun to reflect back the love that was buried within him under all of his pain, guilt, and frustration.

Bargaining

In the bargaining stage, we attempt to change the outcome of our predicament, or at least postpone the inevitable. It is very similar to a child's attempts to control or manipulate circumstances that arise from the boundaries set by parents. When mom or dad won't give in to our temper tantrum, we start to beg and plead. We try to bargain with them by letting them know that we will keep our room clean for a whole week, or that we will never do it again if we just get what it is that we want.

Now, as adults, we turn to God instead of our parents in the belief that somehow God has created this situation and can, therefore, rescue us from death. The plea may be, "If you make me well again, I will go to church every Sunday," or, "If you let me live to see my daughter get married, then I will die in peace." Usually with these requests, there is the promise that we won't ask for more. Yet, if the request is somehow fulfilled, we often forget all about our original promise.

There is often an implicit feeling of guilt intertwined with the bargaining as though somehow, if we had lived life differently, we wouldn't be dying. Thoughts such as "if only I can have" draw us into the future, and thoughts like "if only I had done" hold us to the past. Both of these keep us out of the present. When we stop shifting between these two and turn our attention to the moment, we begin to realize that nothing we try to do is working to change the fact that our body is dying and the world as we know it is slipping away.

Depression

As we turn our attention toward our present condition, a deep sadness runs through us. We are entering the stage of depression. Spiritual teachers have offered the analogy of being in a boat in the middle of a river, where we have left one shore and have not as yet reached the other side. Everything feels dark and gloomy. We know that life is not the way we want it to be, yet, because everything seems to be crumbling around us, we can now see more clearly what is happening in the moment. We dwell in the abyss of our being.

Stephen Levine, in his book *Who Dies?*, sees depression as a confrontation with the truth.[3] He states that, in depression, there is a realization of just how powerless we are. This view stands in contrast to Elisabeth Kubler-Ross' depiction of depression as a more unidimensional reaction to the loss. He writes, "Though many view depression with alarm, a creative process may be going on. We have nowhere to turn; nothing is working in the way we wish. We have come to a place where we are beginning to see how things really might be. Seeing that we cannot control the universe, depression has the power to lead us to a new openness. It is a painful process of shedding the parts of us that are dying away at each moment."[4]

Understanding that depression is, by its very nature, an active and transitional process, we find that the words offered by others are often not very helpful to the person experiencing depression. Rather than calling us to speak, this perspective invites us to simply be. Consider Mary's experience with the depression of a terminally ill patient.

I had been seeing Dave for many weeks. One day I walked into his hospital room and found him lying in bed staring at the ceiling. Anything that I asked him was met with a one-word response. Prior to this visit he had been talkative and friendly, and I felt that we had built a sense of trust and mutual respect. I sat silently for awhile, and then asked him, "Dave, would you like me to leave and come back another time?"

In response, he pleaded, "No, please don't go." Although he didn't wish to talk, as he wrestled with the depths of his being, he also did not want me to leave. I simply sat quietly and meditated. I sensed that he appreciated my presence that day. We didn't need to exchange any words in order to communicate with our hearts.

Never underestimate the power of your peaceful and loving presence. "Being" itself is both healing as well as providing an environment for persons who are dying to move through the depression in their own way and at their own rate. Stephen Levine concludes, "Depression can have almost an alchemical quality about it when we begin to investigate the dross, the fear, the withdrawal, and the anger in our lives and transmute them into a new richness, a deeper understanding. From this understanding a new fearlessness arises, a new loveliness. For some, depression can be an initiation into a new life that is no longer a struggle with difficulty but is instead workable and at last exciting."[5] From here, acceptance naturally emerges.

Acceptance

The feelings of separateness and isolation lift as we gradually move into an acceptance of the changes that we are experiencing as death approaches. When we are willing to be with depression in the way Stephen Levine suggests, it can lead to a new way of being, one filled with excitement and a sense of adventure. In this sense, it is difficult to see acceptance as a stage. There is usually a gradual process of emergence involved rather than the sudden and clearly defined appearance of a stage. We have, for example, seen many individuals simply waiting for death to come. Mary describes a form of acceptance in the following story.

I had been visiting a 101-year-old man in a nursing home. When I would come to see him he would always be sitting in his wheelchair in the hall. George would then tell me about his life in the South. He had been a cook in Chinatown, had never married, and, having been wounded in World War I, received a Purple Heart. Every once in awhile George would ask me, "Why am I still here?" I would inquire to see if he had any unfinished business, but he couldn't think of anything that felt incomplete or undone.

One day when I came to visit, I didn't see him in the hall. As I walked into his room, he was lying in bed. His eyes were closed, his breathing was labored, and in the shadows of his room I saw a nurse who indicated to me that George was dying. I went over to his bed and sat quietly by his side. Shortly thereafter I saw his eyes open slightly. At this point, I asked him, "George, are you leaving us?" He obviously heard me as he pulled himself up on the rail, looked me straight in the eye, and replied, "God, I hope so!"

Although he appeared to be ready and open to dying, there was a subtle struggle or tension in George. One might consider George as someone in the stage of acceptance, but, looking more closely at the subtle tension, he seemed to be more resigned to, than accepting of, the fact that he was going to die and that his only option was to wait. In fact, he lived for three more months following the above episode.

True acceptance is about letting go of the way we expect it to be, the way we believe it should be, or the way we want it to be. It is no longer about clinging to all the things that we had identified with. It is about bringing our awareness into the present and seeing each moment with the eyes and innocence of a child. Is this what Christ meant in Matthew 18:3 when he advised, "Unless you become like little children, you will not enter the Kingdom of Heaven."?[6]

A second illustration of acceptance also comes from Mary's experience: I was once visiting a woman who was close to the end of her life. There was a certain peace that one felt when walking into her room. I would often see a nurse or doctor talking with this woman while taking their break. There was a brightness in her eyes and an openness to what was transpiring in the moment. With that openness, she seemed to bring a freshness and life to those around her. She was willing to be with the unknown including her impending death.

Acceptance is opening to each moment of life, and feeling spacious with what is. By truly opening to life, we are simultaneously letting go of the fear of death. Acceptance is about trusting the process of change, and death represents the single greatest change in life. Ron relates how observing Mary's relationship with her mother helped him in being with his dying father.

I carefully watched Mary's relationship with her mother deepen as they repeatedly talked with each other about their unresolved issues and the unconscious patterns that had affected their relationship over the course of their lives. I truly believe that, because of this work done together, Mary's grief was far less reactive and, in a very real way, purer after the news came of her mother's sudden death.

Having seen the positive results of this process, I then decided that I would share personal feelings with my father who was, at the time, suffering with congestive heart failure, anxiety, diabetes, and a number of lesser ailments in what would turn out to be the last years of his life. At appropriate times in our conversations, I would intentionally and truthfully tell him what a great dad he had been, how much I appreciated and loved him for all that he had done for me, and that he had lived a full and meaningful life. He was aware that his heart was failing and that the end of his life was near.

Over these last years, I noticed his general anxiety level easing as the weeks and months went by, until near the end, he would often say in a relaxed, peaceful, and almost matter-of-fact way, "I am ready to go whenever the good Lord wants to take me." I believe that the words of loving acknowledgment and support that I gave to him during those last years contributed to whatever degree of acceptance he had when his time to die arrived.

When we are in a state of acceptance, there is a realization of a deeper truth. It is a surrendering to the mystery of life itself and an opening to the sacred. True acceptance requires living in the Now.

The following exercise, a guided meditation and visualization, is designed to provide a taste or glimpse of the time of dying.

OPENING TO THE DYING EXPERIENCE: AN EXERCISE

Closing your eyes and sitting with your head, neck, and spine straight, with your feet on the floor, draw your attention from all other places and bring your awareness only to the place where you are sitting. Withdraw your mind from all other times and be aware only of this moment in time. Notice your body, and just feel the weight of it. Bring your awareness to all the sensations in your body as you gently inhale and exhale.

Now, imagine yourself waiting in the doctor's office. You haven't been feeling well, and you are there to talk with the doctor about your test results. The doctor walks in, sits down, and tells you that your x-rays and other test results indicate that you have a terminal illness and probably have only one month left to live. Again, being aware of the sensations in your body and watching your thoughts, notice what comes up for you.

Now imagine that you have only one week to live. What is this like for you? Notice your thoughts and any sensations that may be present.

It is now the last day of your life. What are you aware of? Who is with you? What are you sharing with them?

Now, let yourself die. Open into death. There is nothing to hold on to. Just die gently into this moment. Each breath disappears. Each thought dissolves into space. Not holding on. Letting go of it all. Letting go of the fear. Letting go of the longing. Holding on to nothing. Just let yourself die.

Keeping your eyes closed, become aware of your body once again. When you feel ready, gently open your eyes.[7]

Chapter 3
On Being with Dying

With both death and love, it is the dissolving of boundaries between ourselves and the mystery that loosens the hold of the ego and allows the soul to be revealed.

Ram Dass
Still Here

When we receive a terminal diagnosis, our perspective on life changes radically. We look at who we thought we were and what we identified with in a new way. Possessions, roles, relationships, and careers all fall away. We can no longer take care of ourselves. We cannot drive our car or play with our children. Life continues on without our involvement, and all of our old ways of relating to the world are gone. Perhaps most importantly, life now provides a special opportunity for self-reflection. Mary first noticed this opportunity as a child.

Before she died, my grandmother was bedridden for several years. As a child, I noticed that she seemed deeply contemplative in the silence of her room—an exceptionally authentic and wise woman. Since that time, I have been with many individuals as they journey toward death and have found that, as they open to dying, there are certain recognizable areas where their reflections often lead.

In our culture we often push away pain by keeping ourselves busy. In this way, we avoid feeling and, thereby, knowing what is true for us. When we are dying, however, we tend to turn inward. If we would engage in this self-reflection, resolve our unfinished business, and face the difficult questions regarding life and death now, rather than waiting until we receive our terminal diagnosis, there will be less confusion and unresolved issues, as well as more space for open communication and loving presence, at the end of our lives. Being with dying implicitly entails being with living. In the end, they are inseparably one and the same.

FOUR REFLECTIONS ON LIVING AND DYING

In working with the dying, we have come to recognize four kinds of reflections expressed by those facing the end of their lives, reflections that are consistent with the insights of Christine Longaker.[1] As founder and director of a hospice, her teaching and writing come from her immediate experience, not just from her intellectual understanding.

One's Life and Life's Meaning

Marie-Louise von Franz studied over 60,000 dreams as a student of the renowned psychoanalyst Carl Jung.[2] She found that when people come to the end of their lives, they dream chronologically about their life experiences. She first noticed this pattern in the elderly, but, after studying the dreams of a twelve-year-old girl who was dying of cancer, she noted that this chronological dream sequence seems to occur regardless of one's age.

People who are facing death look back on their lives. We seem to have an innate need to sort out what has been helpful for us from that which we have left unfinished, and, perhaps most notably, to find a purpose in it all. It is helpful, therefore, for those who are terminally ill to talk about both their achievements in life and their regrets.

Unfortunately, it is common to get caught in the cycle of ruminating about what went wrong in life and condemning ourselves for these outcomes. Wrapped in these persistent feelings, we feel powerless to change them. We can, however, actually break this cycle by turning and facing these feelings directly.

The following instructions are meant to be of help in this regard. "Feel the sensations in your body. Allow the feelings to wash over you like a wave without reacting to or obsessively dwelling on them. Simply observe or witness the feelings, and then let them go." When we open in this way, we are letting go of our attachment to the past and being with what is transpiring in the present moment, here and now.

Unresolved Relationships and Other Life Issues

Being at peace with others and completing his or her life's work seem central to the dying person. Finishing business is about letting go of our need to have life be the way we think it should or want it to be. Peace of mind and contentment come when we can be with reality the way it is. Being with what is involves opening our hearts, even when doing so is intensely painful. Mary offers an example of how becoming aware of an unresolved relationship can be important in the dying process.

Bob had been telling me his life story for weeks, and was especially proud of his two children, Laurie and John. He was becoming physically weaker, yet seemed determined to hold on to life. One of his nurses told me that she couldn't understand how he could still be alive with all of the deterioration that had occurred in his body. In talking with her, I discovered that according to his chart he had, not two, but three children.

When I saw him later that day, I said, "Bob, your chart indicates that you have three children. You have told me only about Laurie and John." He was quiet for a while and then slowly told me the story of a second son, Ken, who had, fifteen years before, told him that he was gay. Hearing this, Bob had become enraged and, slamming the door behind him, had told his son that he never wanted to see him again. I asked him how he felt about it now.

With tears in his eyes, he quietly said, "I wish I had never said those things. I wish it had never happened." When I suggested that we find Ken and have him visit, Bob didn't believe that his son would have anything to do with him. Nevertheless, he agreed to the arrangement.

Ken was very pleased that his father wanted to see him. They spoke for quite a while and made a deep and meaningful connection. Bob died peacefully two days later.

Bob was fortunate enough to actually connect with his son before he died, but it is not necessary to meet with the other person in order to resolve emotional pain. There are times when the other is not able or willing to physically meet or is not available emotionally. It is essential for our own peace of mind, however, to at least clear these issues within ourselves.

The first step in this work is having the right intention. It is important to acknowledge the part that we played in creating any painful situation, and to take responsibility for what we said or did in the relationship. Opening our hearts and minds, and being willing to have compassion for both ourselves as well as the other, is immeasurably helpful in resolving the problem. It is also important to enter the conversation without expectations that the other person will change, so that we can be open to whatever happens rather than being unduly influenced by our preconceived notions.

A helpful technique is to focus on the painful problem and to write down everything that comes to you about the situation without judgment or censoring. It may feel awkward and somewhat controlled at first, but as you continue, the thoughts, feelings, and words will begin to flow. Gradually, as thoughts and feelings arise, they will seem to take on a life of their own. Surprising insights will often appear and the rigidity will fall away as a new clarity is revealed. Here is an example from Mary's experience.

Sam was a very affluent businessman before his stroke. In the twelve years since, because the stroke had impaired the functioning of his brain's left hemisphere, he compensated by developing the right side of his brain. During this time, he discovered that he was a talented artist. When it was determined that Sam now had terminal cancer, I was asked to see the family. The doctor gave the task of informing Sam about this diagnosis to his wife, Anne, and she was finding the whole situation simply overwhelming.

In talking with Anne, I learned how grateful she was that she had acknowledged her problem with alcohol and went into recovery just before her husband had the stroke. She now felt that the past twelve years had been very precious, but she didn't know how to face the fact that Sam had cancer. She did not want to be the one to tell him.

As we talked at length, Anne told me that there was something that really bothered her about their relationship. Sam was raised in the Episcopal Church, but had stopped believing in God when he was a young adult. She longed to talk with him about spirituality and life after death but felt blocked in doing so. I suggested that she write him a letter about everything that was on her mind and in her heart without censoring it until she felt complete. I told her that she didn't need to read it to him unless she wished to.

Most of that night was spent writing to him, releasing those feelings that had, in the past, gotten in the way of an open and authentic communication. The following day, Anne was able to see Sam and share her truth with him in a loving and compassionate way. As the intensity of her anxiety and her desire to speak with him about spiritual matters faded, she was able to articulate what she had wanted to say to him for years. To her surprise, he asked to see a priest. In her willingness to work through her fear, she was able to speak with him in a way that he could both feel her heart and open his own.

Stephen Levine says it well. "Finishing business means I open my heart to you, that whatever blocks my heart with resentment or fear, that whatever I still want from you, is let go of and I just send love. I let go of what obstructs our deepest sharing. That I open to you as you are in love. Not as I wish you to be or as I wish me to be. An opening into the oneness beyond the need to settle accounts. No longer looking to be forgiven or to show others how unfair they were. To finish our business, we must begin to stop holding back. Gradually love replaces clinging."[3]

Understanding and Finding Meaning in Suffering

The nature of suffering, and its place in our spiritual journey, become especially important as we near the end of our lives. In those last days, we often contract around the pain that we are experiencing and become puzzled as to why this pain is there. We need to understand its purpose and how it relates to the meaning of life. Mary's childhood experience helped her as an adult to understand the value of suffering.

When I would fall and hurt myself as a child, my mother would compassionately kiss the wound to make the hurt go away. She would then say to me, "Offer it up for the benefit of others." Depending on my mood, and the way in which my mother spoke, those words would feel either soothing and helpful or distancing and dismissing. It wasn't until I was an adult, and went through some very difficult times, that I was able to appreciate the value of these words and hear the wisdom that my mother was expressing. I now see that she was reminding me that what we do in our own minds affects our presence as well as the inner experience of others. In these ways, others can benefit from how we work with our pain. On a practical level, I have also found on repeated occasions that when I did offer my pain to help others with their suffering, the intensity of my own pain eased as well.

Numerous religions and spiritual traditions have spoken of this relationship between the act of dedicating one's pain and the relief of suffering. In the *Tibetan Book of Living and Dying,* for example, Sogyal Rinpoche speaks about a conversation he had with one of his students. "Recently one of my students came to me and said: 'My friend is only twenty-five. He's in pain, and dying of leukemia. He is already frighteningly bitter; I'm terrified that he'll drown in bitterness. He keeps asking me: What can I do with all this useless, horrible suffering?' My heart went out to her and her friend. Perhaps nothing is as painful as believing that there is no use to the pain you are going through. I told my student that there was a way that her friend could transform his death even now, and even in the great pain he was enduring: to dedicate, with all his heart, the suffering of his dying, and his death itself, to the benefit and ultimate happiness of others. I told her to tell him: Imagine all the others in the world who are in a pain like yours, or even greater. Fill your heart with compassion for them. And pray to whomever you believe in and ask that your suffering should help alleviate theirs. Again and again dedicate your pain to the alleviation of their pain. And you will quickly discover in yourself a new source of strength, a compassion you'll hardly be able now to imagine, and a certainty, beyond any shadow of a doubt, that your suffering is not only not being wasted, but has now a marvelous meaning."[4]

When our self-focus shifts by opening our hearts to others, we loosen the grip our mind has on our own pain. Our attachment to the pain lessens and, as our concern for ourself dissipates, we become aware of the underlying unity or connection among all living beings. In this state of being and with this awareness, the dissolving of our own suffering has an actual effect on reducing the suffering of others. Of all the points being presented here, this is the most clearly transpersonal dimension, and, therefore, the most subtle and difficult to describe in words.

Many spiritual traditions speak of the importance of non-attachment. In the Bible, for example, non-attachment or letting go is clearly implied when surrender to the will of God is addressed. The words of Christ are given in Mark 14:36, "Father, Father, everything is possible for you. Take away this cup from me. Yet I want your will, not mine."[5] In 1 John 2:17, it is said, "And this world is fading away ... but whoever keeps doing the will of God will live forever."[6]

The Bhagavad Gita (3:19; 3:25) advises spiritual seekers to be not attached to the fruits of their actions.[7] Every human being experiences both physical and emotional pain. The life of Christ, as well as the lives of many great spiritual masters, had times of intense pain.[8] Yet, as these different traditions teach, the art of non-attachment can lessen the suffering that accompanies the pain.

Joseph Sharp is a minister who has offered pastoral care to the dying for many years. He claims that he did not, however, truly understand their fear and suffering until he received his own life-threatening diagnosis. He writes, "We learn so much through our suffering. Yes, it's painful. Yes, we want it to be over. But it is here, regardless. It is part of our life. We feel it. And the amazing thing that every expert who works with pain tells us is that, once we stop trying to resist our pain, it literally changes texture. Often the pain seems to lessen in intensity. Yet even if it doesn't lessen, the pain nevertheless transforms into something other than 'useless, meaningless' suffering. From here, we can begin to understand pain's larger role in our spiritual development."[9]

Most of us focus on the pleasure of life and do not wish to experience the pain. We would like to keep it as far from our reality as possible. We try to control our lives so that we minimize any painful experiences and enhance the pleasurable ones. It is only when we open to all of life as it presents itself in the moment, that we are more likely to experience the joy that goes beyond our day-to-day experiences—a joy that is much more satisfying than the so-called pleasures of our everyday existence. Letting go and opening to the present moment is actually healing in that our body/ mind is no longer contracting around the fear, the anger, or the need to be seen in a certain way.

The dying process teaches us about letting go. As everything falls away, we are forced to look at both our attractions and aversions. We can learn from the pain by watching what our mind does with it and then noticing the mind's patterns. We see how we contract around pain, and how we suffer because we hold on so dearly to our ideas and expectations of how life should be. When we are dying, we are acutely aware that everything is falling away.

This is an auspicious time for those who wish to deepen their spiritual understanding. This deepening comes when we open to the changes in our lives by observing the mind's tendencies and patterns, and having compassion for ourselves, by simply letting ourselves be authentically who we really are, right here, right now.

Nature and Mystery of Life and Death

As we live our lives, we tend to think about the future and plan for it. The person who is dying also thinks about the future and wonders what it will be like. What will happen after I die? Where will I go? Is there a God and, if so, what is God like? What is it like on the other side? Who will be there? Is there a life after death? The prospect of death brings a focus and a certain sense of urgency to these questions.

Mother Teresa's last words were, "Jesus I love you." When Mahatma Gandhi was shot, his last word was "Ram," a name of God. Mother Teresa and Gandhi were both individuals whose lives were so focused on the divine realm that their minds naturally turned toward God at the time of their death. For those of us who are not as consciously rooted in our spiritual essence, prayer, contemplation, and meditation can be the means that help guide us on our spiritual journey. Hearing familiar sacred words can be both centering and comforting for one who is dying. Mary relates a story from her experience with her dying aunt.

When my Aunt Ann was dying, she lay semi-comatose for three days. Her eyes were closed, and she was unable to communicate. There were only two times that she responded. On one occasion, a priest came to see her, and a smile indicated that she was pleased that he was there. At another time, her face glowed as my brother and I sat by her bed and recited the rosary that she had prayed all of her life.

GUIDELINES FOR BEING WITH THE DYING

As we have emphasized, being in relationship with individuals who are terminally ill is a spiritually auspicious time. From our own experience, we offer three significant guidelines that we have found to be especially important in this context.

1. Be willing to open to one's own inner process. To be fully present with an individual who is dying requires not just intent, but a willingness and skill to look within oneself at each moment to see what is emerging from one's own mind and heart. For most, it is a difficult and, at times, intense experience to be with someone who has a terminal diagnosis. Often awkward feelings arise and we don't know quite what to say or do. We are out of our comfort zone. Observing what is arising within us helps to bring clarity to the situation and deepens our compassion. Our own fear of death often arises, as does the unexpressed grief that we have been unknowingly carrying due to all of the loss and change in our lives.

If the person who is dying is a loved one, we often find that the same patterns of mind that have kept us from communicating openly with this person many times before are once again getting in the way of relating in an open and authentic way during this particular time. In allowing ourselves to experience our own discomfort and painful feelings, we can then watch the contents of our minds and, from this observation, become aware of our previously unconscious mental and emotional habit patterns. In this process, we soon come to realize that we are no different in our essential nature than the weak and fragile person lying in the bed before us. The only difference is that it seems to be that person's turn to leave this world.

2. Be present and listen without expectations. So often our expectations, judgments, and preconceived notions color our thoughts, words, and actions when we are with another. We constantly, and without much awareness, filter their experience through our own matrix of thoughts and feelings and, thereby, end up not really hearing or understanding the experience that they are attempting to describe. In the more extreme cases, frustration results, and both individuals fall silent, feeling unable to communicate what they are really thinking and feeling.

To be truly present, one must learn to recognize one's own inner voices and not allow them to interfere, color, and distort one's immediate, direct perception of what the other person is actually expressing. We need to truly "get" what the other is saying. With practice, one can thereby learn to simply be with the other and remain relatively unaffected, in a reactive way, by what they might say or do. As one stays present with the other's experience as well as with one's own, a sharpened intuitive sense and feeling of inspiration begin to arise from a deeper level within.

3. Provide a non-judging and non-reactive space for the unfolding of the other's process of spiritual growth and self-transformation. It has been said that returning to God or the source of our being is the true purpose of human existence. In contrast to this, many of us have been raised in this culture believing that the core of our being is worthless or bad in some way, and that we have to actively work to gain any sense of goodness or self-respect.

Yet, spirit is our essence and we naturally seek to understand and integrate our worldly experiences with this as our ground. We are a spiritual being first and it is only with this inner foundation that we live in the world of forms. It is not a matter of doing anything. It is truly a matter of being, and coming from that sacred place whenever we speak or act.

If we remain aware of this while relating to the person who is dying, our very state of being serves as a living reminder of this sacred place. Our presence itself will resonate with and, thereby, evoke, the sacred or soul essence in the other. The spirit in each of us is naturally drawn to reunite with the spirit in others. In this way, both individuals can co-create a more authentic and fulfilling relationship.

ON THE NEED TO PREDICT AND CONTROL

Given our fear of death and the resultant need to control the changes inherent in life, we tend to approach the dying process with a belief that, if we're sensitive enough and use the right techniques, we will know what steps to take at what time and be able to predict what will happen next. This need to structure the inherently mysterious and unpredictable process of dying, and to live in the illusion that we really know what is going on, is designed to reduce our anxiety and fear of the unknown.

We have come to realize that there is no right way to die. Each of us must experience the process as it unfolds, being careful not to compare our own experiences and reactions to those of others, and not to be swayed unnecessarily by the even well-meaning advice of loved ones or any others who feel they know what's best. Anxiety often works in very subtle ways when dying is at hand. In the face of this anxiety, it is difficult to remember that each person, when the time comes to cross that line from life into death, must cross that line alone. The following two stories are from Ron's work with the dying.

Edward was a practicing Sufi who had recently been diagnosed with AIDS. He had asked a friend, Beth, if she knew anyone who was familiar with Stephen Levine's approach to dying and who would be willing to guide him in a conscious way when his time of dying came.

Beth introduced us, and for the next several months Edward and I talked in great detail about how he would like to be guided and exactly what he would like me to say at the time of his dying. A long-time meditator, he seemed deeply committed to his spiritual life and quietly confident regarding the part that death would play in his spiritual journey. If ever I had met someone who would die peacefully without fear, Edward was that person.

One evening I was at home washing the dishes after dinner when the phone rang. It was Beth who informed me that Edward had taken a serious turn for the worse and was, in fact, near death. If I wanted to see him again, I had better see him now. Given my commitment to him, I dropped everything and quickly drove to the hospital where he had been undergoing tests for the past few days.

When I arrived, I found him on a gurney in line behind two other patients, each waiting their turn to enter the CAT-Scan machine. His eyes were closed, he seemed semi-comatose, and his breathing evidenced the tell-tale "rattle" that often characterizes the breath of a person shortly before they die. What Beth had said in our brief phone conversation seemed to be true. He seemed very close to death.

I sat down next to him, oblivious to my surroundings, and began to guide him in the way that he had requested and that we had practiced many times in the past four months. I spoke softly for nearly forty-five minutes as his gurney inched along in line. It was now 11 P.M. Edward had not spoken a word or opened his eyes. He remained essentially unchanged. The only thing

I had noticed, but had not given much attention or meaning to at the time, was that he would sharply twitch his right hand and arm on several different occasions during the time that I was guiding him.

I did not know quite what to do at this point. Edward did not die, but still seemed very close to death. So, I started again and went through the entire guided process for a second time. Once again, except for the occasional twitching of his hand and arm, he remained still, eyes closed, silent, and breathing with great effort. It was now past midnight and the medical staff indicated that I had to leave since it was Edward's turn to enter the CAT-Scan apparatus. Not seeing any other option at this point, I went home.

The next morning I received a phone call from Beth who proceeded to tell me that Edward had made a remarkable recovery, was back in his hospital bed, and was alert and talking. I was happily surprised to hear this unexpected news and again dropped everything and drove down to the hospital.

When I entered his room, I found Edward sitting up in bed watching television. I recall feeling how wonderful it was to see him alive and awake once again, but when I greeted him and expressed my joy in seeing him, I received nothing in reply. His eyes stayed locked on the TV set. He wouldn't acknowledge my words or my presence—absolute silence! Another attempt or two to interact with him met with similar results—no acknowledgment or response of any kind.

Feeling awkward, hurt, shocked, and not knowing what to say or do next, I finally decided to leave. I said good-bye and began to leave the room. Just as I was about to step out into the hallway, a very loud and powerful voice said "Stop!" I stopped and slowly turned around. Without taking his eyes off of the television screen, and in a very clear voice, Edward said, "I never want to hear that Stephen Levine bullshit again!" Suddenly, the jerking movements of his hand and arm that I had noticed the night before took on a new meaning. It seems that when the time actually came to walk consciously and calmly through death's door, Edward's resistance, reactivity, and desire to remain alive took center stage, covering up any other inclinations toward peace, love, and surrender that may have been there.

This was the last time that I saw Edward, and he never called again. I later heard that he had died the following week in the middle of the night, alone and angry. Given the man I had come to know, this is not the way I had expected Edward to leave this world.

My Aunt Alma was a very warm and loving, yet reactive and emotional woman. Growing up through my childhood and teenage years in northern New Jersey, it seemed that she was always feeling strongly about someone or something. Peace of mind was not something she seemed to experience for very long. Although she could be quietly comforting on occasions, her personality was simply too fiery for her mind to truly rest.

In the early 1990s I received a phone call from Aunt Alma's husband, my Uncle Harry, who informed me that she had been hospitalized with abdominal pain, and had received a diagnosis of terminal cancer. Aunt Alma was dying and did not have long to live.

Rather than flying back to the East Coast from California to see her, I decided to phone her instead. When I phoned and asked to speak to my aunt, a nurse informed me that he would have to be with her in order to hold the phone to her ear. She was too weak to hold it herself. Preparing myself inwardly for Aunt Alma's usual emotionally colored response, I said, "Hello Aunt Alma. How are you?" Much to my pleasant surprise, and after a long moment of silence, she replied in an even and calm voice, "Hi Ronny [my childhood family name], I'm dying." I could not remember, in all the years that I had known my aunt, her ever speaking in such a profoundly peaceful, direct, and confident manner.

I must admit that my first thought was that she was heavily medicated and was not fully herself at that time (I later found out that that was not the case). Continuing our conversation, I then asked her, "Are you afraid?" Again after a period of silence, she replied with the same peace and calm, "No. We all have to die sometime." Before I could speak again, she continued, "I am, however, concerned about your Uncle Harry. He's not doing very well with all of this." I assured her that we would take care of him and that she need not worry "I'm very tired. I need to go now. I love you Ronny." Now with tears flowing, I replied, "I love you too Aunt Alma." The next voice was that of the nurse ending the call as he hung up the phone. Two days later, Uncle Harry called to tell me that Aunt Alma had died. Here is an instance of a remarkable change in someone who became quieter and less afraid as death approached.

Although we tend to die the way we lived, the truth is that you never know how someone will be in their final hours.

Chapter 4
Grief and the Grieving Process

Grief drives us into habits of serious reflection, sharpens the understanding,
and softens the heart.
John Adams
letter to Thomas Jefferson, May 6, 1816

Many years ago, Mary attended a workshop given by Stephen and Ondrea Levine. Stephen offered an insight that she experienced as quite profound, personally transforming, and extremely valuable in her own work with those dying and grieving. He said, "All emotional pain is grief." Since that time, we have found this statement to be consistently true in our attempts to understand and integrate the emotional pain that we encounter. We find that we have greater compassion for ourselves and others when we see emotional pain as a manifestation of grief.

No matter what it is that we are feeling, if we turn and go back into the emotion, we eventually find its source in a loss of some kind. Grief is a result of how we relate to this change in our lives, whether it be an actual loss or just the fear of loss. We grieve because we become emotionally attached to people, places, things, and ideas. We had identified with the loved one who is now gone, the object that we have lost, or the belief that we had. When a person to whom we have become attached dies or when we receive the diagnosis of a terminal illness, we question who we are and what life is about. Our identity shifts and our perception and experience of life change.

In the present context, our focus is primarily on the grief we experience when a loved one dies, but anytime we experience a great loss, whether it be through a divorce, the loss of a job, our house burning down, or our own impending death, there is grief. Even in apparently pleasant and joyful situations, such as a wedding, graduation, a birthday, or the birth of a child, there is an underlying pain related to the grief we experience over that which has changed. Whenever there is grief, there is also the opportunity to open to that sacred place that is within us all.

Numerous authors have attempted to describe the specific nature of the grieving process, each of them writing from his or her own perspective.[1] Although influenced by these different perspectives, our approach is primarily based on our own experience. While addressing the similarities or common elements in the grieving process throughout this chapter, we also recognize that each person's experience of the grieving process is quite unique.

We have chosen to focus on the foundational work of Elisabeth Kubler-Ross and the contributions of William Lamers, M.D. who has devoted much of his personal and professional life to hospice work. He currently serves as a consultant to the Hospice Foundation of America. We are especially drawn to the work of these particular individuals because their models are both process-oriented, as well as easily adapted to addressing the transformative nature of dying and grieving. In Chapter 2, we described Kubler-Ross' five stages of dying. If all emotional pain is grief, then the five stages of dying, which are characterized by emotional responses of various kinds, are also, therefore, the five stages of grieving. This is the process that we experience in order to let go of whatever we are attached to.

Kubler-Ross says that we actually go through these stages several times a day.[2] The loss, and the grieving process that follows, may involve a small thing that happens in a split second or something that is very traumatic and can take years to move through. She asks us to imagine being intensely involved in reading an interesting book when the telephone rings. What is the first thing we do? We deny that the phone is ringing. We may say something like, "That can't be the phone!" Next comes a feeling of anger and frustration. We may say, "Who on earth can that be?" Bargaining usually follows. "Well, let me just read one more line!" Then comes the depression, [after a long sigh] "I'd better see who it is." You then answer the phone and find that it is a dear friend. "Oh, hello Sarah, how are you?" You have now completely forgotten about the book, accepting the fact that you were interrupted.

This whole process can take as little as two or three rings of the phone. Denial, anger, bargaining, depression, and acceptance are all aspects of the process that we encounter as we let go of whatever we are attached to. We are actually grieving much of the time without even realizing it.

When we are dying, we are grieving. We are losing everything we have on this level of reality. We are losing our loved ones, our career, all of our possessions, and our ability to function. We are losing our health and finally our bodies. We are losing everything and everyone that we have known while living on this earth.

It is also true that when we are grieving, we are dying. We are dying to who we thought we were, and to what we have identified with for so long. That which was a part of us is now gone. As we let go of our attachments, only then do we die back into the spiritual identification that we have forgotten.

William Lamers uses a Grief Wheel to describe the grieving process.[3] The Grief Wheel, shown in Figure 1, describes a process that is similar, but not identical, to Kubler-Ross' description of the five stages.

Both Lamers and Kubler-Ross acknowledge that shock and denial are the first experiences in an unfolding and painful process of letting go of our attachments. As you can see, the Grief Wheel incorporates Kubler-Ross' stages of denial, anger, and depression. Acceptance, though not actually mentioned in Lamer's model, is implicit in the phases of reorganization and recovery. The only stage not addressed in any noticeable way is bargaining.

Bargaining happens more in the anticipation of the loss. It also occurs, however, in the grief that results from the actual loss itself. For instance, Stephen Levine recounts conversing with a woman whose child had died. She described her situation. "I gave his clothes away to a home for orphaned children. But when I packed them up, it was so terribly hard I had to say to myself, 'O.K. If he comes back, I'll buy him new clothes.'"[4]

Regardless of how we label the experiences that we have when grieving, we each go through the process in our own individual way. Remember that the grieving process is not purely linear; grief comes in waves, spirals, and, as we see with the Grief Wheel, is cyclical in nature. As we open to our painful feelings, and we gradually bring them into awareness, the process becomes a spiritual journey, as we learn more about our true Self each step of the way. In this way, we are being more true to who we are. This process is both expansive and satisfying.

We have come to see the grieving process as evolving in three discernable, yet overlapping, phases that successively emerge as the process unfolds: Resistance and Protest, Realization and Integration, and Acceptance and Transformation. Let us look at each of these in turn.

RESISTANCE AND PROTEST

Stephen Levine writes in *Who Dies?*, "If you are trying to be someone doing something, controlling the flow, then when that which is uncontrollable approaches, your resistance becomes greater and your suffering more intense."[5] We don't want to hear that our loved one has just died, or that we have a terminal illness, or that whatever it is we are attached to will no longer be there for us. Our whole system resists the news and we protest. This resistance and protest is often not even conscious. A powerful experience in Ron's personal life lends support to this insight.

I was sitting in the dining room reading a new book when the phone rang. The voice on the phone said that she was a neighbor of my parents, and that my father had asked her to call me. The voice continued to tell me that my mother had been found lying unconscious in the front seat of her car in her closed garage with the car engine running, and had just been taken by ambulance to the local hospital. I felt cold, heavy, and numb. Time had somehow stopped.

Yet, in this state, I drove to the hospital with my wife and two-year-old son, and arrived just in time to watch the paramedics wheel my mother, who was covered with a sheet on a portable stretcher, into the hospital's emergency room. I walked into the hospital and was directed to a room where my father was waiting. As I walked towards him, I noticed that his face was white and his whole body was trembling. I put my arm around him and we talked quietly for awhile, already knowing what news we were about to hear. After waiting about thirty minutes, a doctor entered the room where we were sitting and informed us that, despite all of their efforts to revive her, my mother had died.

Shock and Denial

When we first hear the news that our loved one has died, our reaction is to shut it out. We often go into shock and feel numb. Shock is actually an important protection, while denial is the psycho-emotional reaction to the loss, and is almost always deeply intertwined with the shock. We attempt to go on with our lives as if nothing has happened. Our attachment to the person and resistance to the pain may be so intense that, without the shock to buffer the reality of the loss, we ourselves might die as a result.

Shock and denial are nature's ways of providing time for us to gradually absorb the news, and begin to integrate what has occurred. It is common, for example, that, a week after the funeral, a woman will be thinking about her husband's death while, at the same time, setting the dinner table for him.

Our life can feel very confusing during the time of grieving. Poor concentration, memory loss, and experiencing daily life as surreal begin to feel like the norm. It is important, therefore, that people know about the grieving process in order to minimize the feeling that they may be losing their minds.

The shock that we experience can last from moments, as in Kubler-Ross' example of the telephone call, to months or even years, depending on how strong the attachment is. It is not unusual, for example, for a parent to go in and out of shock and denial for up to two years after their child has died. Here is an example from Mary's personal experience.

My daughter Debbie was pregnant when my son Ted died in a motorcycle accident. He had really been looking forward to Debbie's baby being born. Three months after Ted died, my son-in-law called during the night to tell me that my granddaughter, Patiance, had been born. I was very excited! I decided to wait until the morning to tell the family in order not to awaken them. The first thing on my mind when I woke up was that I was a grandmother. I quickly went to Ted's room and knocked on the door. I knew how excited he would be. He didn't open the door, so I called for him. He didn't answer. When I opened the door to tell him and saw that the room was empty, it was as though I had heard the news of his death for the first time. From that experience, a whole new level of reality began to open.

The physical manifestations of shock include feelings of numbness, heaviness, and exhaustion. Sighing and shortness of breath may occur. Often one gains or loses weight, and has difficulty sleeping. A more complete list of the physical effects of grieving, as well as lists of the behavioral, cognitive, emotional, and spiritual effects are given in Figure 2. Mary continues.

When my son died, I experienced all of these effects, yet, on another level, I could feel that I was moving towards a deeper understanding of love and of life itself. When I first heard of Ted's death, I remember making the decision that, if I had to go through the pain of this loss, I would use this time as a spiritual journey. I wrote and talked about my experience, investigated my dreams, did collage work, and meditated and prayed, continually examining the pain as it presented itself. There were days that I would sob, and then there would be a clearing, when the grass was an intensely beautiful green and the sky was an incredible blue. In moments of feeling so much love and so much pain at the same time, I felt very alive. Surrendering to the magnitude of the mystery of life and death, I was aware of and felt an unseen presence guiding me through this process. It felt as though I was being held.

During such times, reality itself often seems to change. One may, for example, experience meaningful events that occur simultaneously or in close sequence without any causal or logical connection. Carl Jung coined the term "synchronicity" to describe experiences of this kind.[6] Mary's experience with synchronicity is related in the following excerpt from her journal.

I could see the many synchronicities that were now taking place in my life, and could feel the guidance and the flow of life in these various experiences. For instance, on the day of the funeral, it was late in the afternoon and friends and relatives had gathered at our house. After talking with a friend who had come to the funeral, I thought to myself, "I haven't eaten all day. I probably should eat something." Just then someone handed me a plate of food. I then talked for another ten minutes and I thought, "I don't have a fork," and someone handed me a fork. These kind of events happened over and over again. My heart was broken open and I was being shown a whole new dimension of being.

Such experiences involve a deeper seeing from which a new understanding of life may emerge. Mary goes on to describe the personal transformations that she observed in herself.

Throughout the first few years after Ted's death, life was extremely difficult. Within the first months, I felt open and vulnerable. It seemed so intense that all I could do was surrender to the process. I felt humble as the waves of pain washed over me. The less I resisted my painful experience, the more life flowed. I was a substance abuse counselor at the time, and part of my job was working with individuals in crisis. I found myself being with these clients in a transformative way that was surprising to both my employer and to myself. I found that by letting go of what I had no power to change, I became more open to the sacredness of life. My mere presence affected others in powerful ways. Many clients felt healed just by talking with me. For that period of time, I was so open to the pain and so surrendered to the process, that life just flowed through me.

Fear and Anxiety

Panic set in as Bob found out that his wife had died in surgery. "Everyone was moving in slow motion. I could see people speaking, but I couldn't make out what they were saying. How can I live without her? She is my world, my life. What will I tell my children? What will I tell myself?"

Fear grips us at times. We may fear that we will forget what our loved one looked like or that we can't continue without him or her. We may also fear that other loved ones will die. Anxiety may come from seemingly nowhere. We feel restless and want to do something, anything, to avoid the pain. One of our students expressed the process that she went through in opening to her fear after a marital divorce, and what she learned about dying from this process.

I have been avoiding the pain of separation and the fear of stepping into the unknown. The fear of being alone is something that I will probably have to contend with when I am dying. Where do I go when my body dies? Do I go someplace all alone? I imagine that the threshold of stepping into that absolute unknown of death is in some way similar to the stepping into the uncertainty of the world as I leave this home and relationship. I do not, however, live in fear all the time. There are moments when I truly am able to trust the organic process of separation. There is a part of me that knows I do not have to push or force anything because the right time will present itself. After journaling or meditating, I am sometimes able to contact this place and know that there is a bigger movement that I am part of. The backdrop of this bigger movement of life helps me hold the relationship more softly, with less grasping.

Whatever fears may arise in our minds, if we turn and face them, and travel back to their source, we find that all fears are rooted in the fear of death. Said another way, if we truly open to dying and accept it on all levels in our lives, all other fears dissolve. People who are most afraid to live are those who are most fearful of dying, and those who are terrified of death are often those who resist fully experiencing life.

Death appears in many forms—as part of changes we experience in our daily lives, the death of a loved one, or when confronting our own mortality. In whatever context it occurs, death has the potential of breaking us open and helping us loosen our grip on life so that we can live more fully.

In his book, *The Way to Love,* Anthony de Mello writes, "Has it ever struck you that those who most fear to die are the ones who most fear to live? That in running away from death we are running away from life? Think of a man living in an attic, a little hole of a place with no light and little ventilation. He fears to come down the stairs because he has heard of people falling down stairs and breaking their necks. He would never cross a street because he has heard of thousands who have been run over on the streets. And, of course, if he cannot cross a street, how will he cross an ocean or a continent or one world of ideas to another? This man clings to his hole of an attic in the attempts to ward off death and in doing so he has simultaneously warded off life. What is death? A loss, a disappearance, a letting go, a saying good-bye. When you cling, you refuse to let go, you refuse to say good-bye, you resist death. And even though you may not realize it, that is when you resist life too. For life is on the move and you are stuck, life flows and you have become stagnant, life is flexible and free and you are rigid and frozen. Life carries all things away and you crave for stability and permanence. So you fear life and you fear death because you cling. When you cling to nothing, when you have no fear of losing anything, then you are free to flow like the mountain stream that is always fresh and sparkling and alive."[7]

Anger

Anger can come in many forms. Initially we may react by screaming or crying in disbelief, and later in the process feel irritated or frustrated as the reality settles in. It is a way of protesting the loss. We want to blame and lash out at anyone who is around.

There is an undercurrent of feelings beneath the anger. Our world seems as though it is crumbling. We feel helpless and out of control. "Why did this happen?" is the question that inevitably comes up. Fear, disappointment, feelings of guilt, and the frustration of not getting what we want are just beneath the surface. We feel unloved and unappreciated. "How can this be happening?" "This just isn't fair!" "The doctor should/shouldn't have operated." No answer satisfies us. Often we are surprised to discover how intense and irrational the anger can be. In this regard, Mary speaks about a humbling experience in her life.

I remember my sister-in-law criticizing my mother at my brother's funeral. Jimmy died when I was twenty-seven years old in a motorcycle accident and I hadn't realized how angry I was about his death. When I heard my sister-in-law criticizing my mother, the anger that had been bubbling up in me since I heard about the accident all came out on her. I was so enraged that I left my body. A part of me was above my body watching with great curiosity, very detached, looking down and seeing this person down below being enraged at her sister-in-law. I had not realized at that time that this rage sprang from the unexpressed grief over my brother's death. This anger served as an emotional release for my general frustration and feelings of powerlessness. Later when I realized what the rage was really about, I apologized to her.

It is important to have patience and compassion for both ourselves and others when we are grieving. When we are angry, we want things to be the way they were. We feel frustrated and may not even realize that the anger has anything to do with grief. We may project our anger onto the doctor, the nurses, God, or our loved ones. We often hold on to this anger, as it feels energizing and keeps us from sinking into the sadness.

There are, however, ways that one can defuse the anger rather than waiting until it becomes so intense that we lash out at others. Journaling, for example, can help to soften and bring clarity to the anger. One of our clients actually bought a set of inexpensive dishes, and threw them against a wall behind her house in order to express and release her anger. A similar experience comes from Mary's personal journal.

Several weeks after my brother Jimmy's death, I found myself with a pile of laundry and just not wanting to do the wash. I had recently heard that it was helpful to hit a pillow and name the things that you are angry at. I thought I would try it on this pile of laundry. No sooner had I started then I found myself yelling out Jimmy's name. I was stunned! How could I be angry with Jimmy? He didn't want to die! I have since learned that people often will not admit to themselves that they are angry with their loved one for dying because, in most instances involving illness or an accident, these angry feelings are seen as unreasonable, illogical, or just not making any sense.

When someone else's anger is directed at you, a new challenge presents itself. Rather than taking the anger personally and reacting, we can be present to what is emerging. Being with and opening to the emotions that are in the room, both our own and the other person's, we may come to see the pain that the other person is unable to acknowledge, the fear and frustration resulting from the change that they are going through. We can also see the painful emotions that are arising within us, including our own unexpressed grief. By being present and letting the emotions quiet down, we can see more clearly what is there.

Guilt and Bargaining

Feelings of guilt are more predominant when one is grieving a loss that has already occurred, whereas bargaining is more evident prior to the loss itself. Guilty feelings are all too common and are portrayed in many ways. Some feel them mildly, while others are obsessed by them. We might feel guilty for something we said or didn't say, or did or didn't do. We may believe that somehow we could have prevented our loved one's death, prolonged his or her life, or somehow made the dying process easier and less painful. Usually we don't even think of these things when the person is alive, but they can haunt us after the person dies. Here is an example from Mary's childhood.

When I was twelve years old, my grandmother died. One evening, shortly before her death, she wanted to teach me French. I wasn't interested in learning French; I just wanted to watch TV. After her death, I felt guilty that I didn't allow her to teach me her native language. It was a persistent dull pain, vacillating between anxiety and loneliness, that literally gnawed at me.

Embarrassment may occur along with feelings of guilt and self-blame, and so we find it hard to talk about our feelings or even admit them to ourselves. Sometimes it is our unconscious guilt that is projected onto others as blame. When we don't open to and express the pain, the feelings remain unresolved. By exploring these feelings, we can discover what lies beneath them. We begin to see how we have unnecessarily taken on responsibility for what has occurred. Guilt often serves as an unconscious defense designed to push away and deny what is. This defense keeps us from being in the present.

The experience of feeling guilty thus keeps death at a distance. The feeling of guilt itself is based on the mistaken belief that we can control the dying process by believing that the death could have been delayed or avoided if only we had or had not done something. When we feel guilty, we do not tell ourselves the truth that our loved one's death was unavoidable no matter what we did or did not do. We turn away from what is real. In this way, guilt is laced with denial, and, unlike anger, does not feel energizing. In fact, we feel depleted and less powerful when we turn the blame on ourselves.

Guilt takes different forms in different contexts. If deep and painful guilt feelings have some logical, real-world basis, such as those of the man who lost his whole family because he had been drinking and driving, it is especially important for such individuals to integrate their powerful experiences with compassion and, at least some degree of, self-forgiveness.

Survivor's guilt is another relatively common form. In a war, accident, or other disaster, such as an earthquake or flood where the person grieving was involved in the incident but did not die, the survivor often feels guilty that he or she lived through it while the other person did not.

Lastly, there is the guilt associated with an inheritance, or somehow having an easier and less complicated life, because our loved one has died. Often a person will spend their inheritance quickly and carelessly in an attempt to eliminate the uncomfortable feelings, or an individual may feel guilty because they now feel relieved that the daily demands of caring for the dying person are gone. Professional counseling and/or group support is appropriate in all of these situations.

As mentioned above, bargaining is more likely to occur when one is anticipating a loss. Kubler-Ross sees bargaining as having three components: a desire, a deadline, and a promise that we won't ask for more.[8] As an example, consider the daughter whose mother was dying of cancer. Addressing God, the daughter said, "God, just let Mom live long enough to attend my wedding." After the daughter married, she asked if her mother could live until her baby was born. In this way, the bargaining often goes on and on. Bargaining is a way of trying to control our world when it feels like the world is collapsing around us. We don't want the impending loss to occur, so we try to control the situation without realizing that this is what we are doing. With the actual loss, there is less of a tendency to bargain, but it still appears on occasion.

Mary relates how she found herself bargaining after her son's death.

Each night I would bargain with God to give me just one more dream about Ted and then I would be okay. When I did dream about him, I was so happy to see him, even though when I faced the reality of his absence in the morning, I was once again emotionally devastated. The pain came in waves. Yet, I always wanted just one more dream.

In both cases, impending loss or actual loss, our defenses are not usually conscious. Both feelings of guilt and bargaining keep us from being present in the moment. Guilt keeps us stuck in the past, while bargaining keeps us focused on the future. Anxiety arises as the denial begins to crumble, and so we turn to bargaining in our attempts to shut out the reality of the loss.

When someone we love dies, or when we anticipate the death of a loved one, our lives begin to unravel. We want to believe that somehow we could have kept, or can now keep, the loss from happening. It is frightening to realize, especially when faced with the inevitability of death, that we have so little control over what happens in our lives. We desperately want to feel secure and to believe that everything is manageable.

REALIZATION AND INTEGRATION

After the resistance and protesting, the reality of the loss becomes more and more apparent as the resistance and protest no longer defend us from the pain of the loss. We start to realize that what had seemingly been a permanent part of our lives is now gone. As time passes and we begin to adjust to life without our loved one, we start to experience death on a more cellular level. Life is changing and, even though we don't like it, our lives are now very different.

The grieving process does not easily lend itself to a linear interpretation. It is like mercury. If you have ever broken a thermometer and tried to scoop up the mercury, you know how difficult it is to pick up the pieces. The shape of the mercury is constantly shifting and changing. Grieving is like that. Anytime we attempt to describe the grieving process in terms of components or categories, we soon realize that it is not easily amenable to being described in a clear and predictable way.

Starting from the moment that we first become aware of the loss, a process of realization and integration of the change in our lives begins. It is only after trying to dismiss or avoid the reality of the loss by resisting and protesting that realization and integration become more predominant. We gradually realize that we cannot bring our loved one back. Therese Rando, in *Treatment of Complicated Mourning,* comments on this process. "It is only when continual frustration of yearning and searching for the deceased brings the mourner to the conclusion that the loss is permanent and irrevocable, and there is consequent abandonment of the search for the deceased, that disorganization, despair, and depression set in. Prior to that, there exists, at least deep in the mourner's mind, the belief that the deceased can be recovered."[9]

Disorientation

When we feel that our lives are shifting so suddenly and drastically, we feel lonely and disconnected, out of synch with the rest of the world. These are all forms of disorientation. Loneliness is common when we lose our physical and emotional contact with those we loved. We miss their form. Feeling lonely indicates that we are more fully aware of the loss. We are starting to let the truth settle in.

Carol was grappling for words as she tried to describe how disoriented she felt after her husband died. "Have you ever had a project and the project ends, and you have invested a lot of time and energy into the project? You feel lost and adrift. You don't know where you are going to go from here. You have left one shore and have not reached the other. You know the feeling? You can kind of see glimpses of the other shore at times, but it still seems far off!"

This often happens with grief. We feel disoriented, lost, and disorganized. We simply cannot get our thoughts together or concentrate on anything. We begin to ask questions like, "Who am I without this person?" "What is my purpose in life without him?" "How am I going to live without her?" We feel adrift until we finally shift our perception and slowly become more accepting of the loss, eventually finding our center again. Disorientation eases as the realization deepens and we begin to confront the truth.

Depression

There is a deep sadness and a turning inward in grieving that is often labeled as depression. It is common for depression that occurs as part of the grieving process to be misunderstood and mistaken for a clinical depression by both professionals and lay persons alike, as in this example from Mary's life.

Many years ago, I was counseling a high school teacher, a woman whose teenage daughter had died. She told me that she no longer wanted to be here. I assessed her to see if she was suicidal. I asked her if she had ever attempted suicide before, if there was any family background of suicide, and whether or not she now felt like taking her life. Somewhat shocked by my questions, she said to me, "I don't want to kill myself; I just want to be with my child." We continued to meet for several months until she returned to her teaching position. At this point, I referred her to a therapist whose office was closer to her home. She later came to a grief support group that I was facilitating and told me that she had informed her therapist (as she had earlier told me) that she no longer wanted to be here. Her therapist reacted by having her admitted to a psychiatric hospital, fearing that she was suicidal.

She told me that she learned to "play the game" during her enforced hospital stay, and, only then, did they release her. She didn't want to take her life; she just wanted to be with her child.

Unlike clinical depression, the depression that occurs while one is grieving is a more natural response. As shown in Figure 3, some aspects of clinical depression are similar to those of grief-related depression, while others are distinctly different. In both cases the individual tends to go within and withdraw, with an accompanying general loss of interest in life. The central difference worth noting is that in grief-related depression the person wants to be with their loved one. The depression is clearly a result of the loss, and the person is preoccupied with that loss. In clinical depression, the preoccupation tends to be with oneself, often focusing on one's badness, failure, lack of worth, hopelessness, and other negative thoughts.

Depression can be a great teacher. In her article on the spiritual gifts of depression, Joanne Blum writes, "As I think back on the serious depressions of my life, I realize that all of the growth spurts in my spiritual life have come from those dark sojourns—and the grace that brought me through them. Perhaps it is especially in hell that we learn that God's grace is with us because we must dive deep for it, because we are motivated to raise our voices and ask for it, and because we finally have enough empty space within, vacated by our egotistical all-knowingness, to receive it."[10]

David Rosen also writes about depression as part of the sacred journey. He emphasizes the importance of killing the false self in a symbolic death. He states, "Depression is a frightening transitional phase characterized by a death-rebirth struggle. In time, the individual contacts the center of the psyche leading to a reorganization of the ego and the emergence of the *true self* (genuine being)."[11] He goes on to say that most theorists in psychology and psychiatry see depression as something negative, but he, much like Carl Jung, sees depression as a potentially favorable affect linked to the quest for meaning. "Depression is a natural reaction to a disruptive situation and is essential for the psyche to adapt. It can also be regarded as a dark, underground process where seeds of new life germinate."[12]

Depression can, at times, lead to the anguish of despair. Sometimes it is difficult to believe that life can ever be pleasant again after our loved one has died. Yet, allowing the process to unfold, we can go beyond our egocentric identity and find a deeper part of ourselves, that part that is connected to something greater than our worldly identity.

Depression is a necessary part of the grieving process. It is a confrontation with the truth of what is.[13] This confrontation goes much deeper, however, than just the truth that our loved one is gone. We are confronted with the truth of ourselves. All the unconscious patterns that have kept us from truly being alive and present to the mystery of life are magnified in the experience of grief. When we can allow this process to flow through us, we can find the joy that goes beyond pleasure and pain.

Resignation

As our awareness of the loss becomes more acute, we start to resign ourselves to the fact that our loved one has died. There is still a void. Some may want to fill the void by becoming more engaged with work or activity. Others may withdraw and want to be alone. The intensity of the grief starts to die down. We don't feel as frantic and disoriented, yet our interest in life hasn't yet fully returned. We may even wonder if our love for the one who has died has diminished since we are no longer deep in sorrow.

Kubler-Ross doesn't really address the issue of resignation, at least not in a formally recognized way. Levine, however, feels that much of what Kubler-Ross meant by the word acceptance was, in fact, actually a form of resignation. He points out, "In the word 'resignation' we see the concept of a re-signing, of a recommitment, a new contract with life made possible as we open to our fear of dying as well as living."[14] In this way, resignation can be seen as an essential step that connects depression to the realm of true acceptance.

ACCEPTANCE AND TRANSFORMATION

As we let ourselves experience the pain of the death of our loved one, our perception of ourselves and our world shifts. When a person whom we love dies, a part of us dies as well. As a result, this forces us to take a deeper look at who we are and at our relationship with life. Often we question the meaning of life and death, and wonder what it will be like after we die or if, in fact, there is a life after death.

As the pain of grief diminishes and we become increasingly accepting, we notice that life takes on a new meaning. We no longer constantly think about our loss. Even when we do think of the loss, and feel the related emotions, they no longer come with the intense pain that had haunted us before. Our values shift and we discover a new enthusiasm for life. Friendships change and deepen. We become less interested in socializing and materially oriented activities, and more interested in love, compassion, and helping relationships. We become more authentic.[15]

Stephen Levine reflects on the dramatic changes that occur in the grieving process. He tells us that, "These are the stages of passing from heaven to hell, from resistance to acceptance. These are the stages of converting our predicament from tragedy to grace, from confusion to insight and wisdom, from agitation to clarity. They are our pilgrimage toward the truth, the process we go through confronting the loss of some security that we can no longer run to for reassurance."[16]

Letting Go of Attachment

Grief has the power to break us open in a way that reveals our mind's deepest holdings and attachments. There are very few other recognized human experiences that rip away the veil quite like grief. To the extent that we are attached is the extent that we remain trapped at a superficial level, trying to control our environment, feeling rigid, afraid, and confused, wanting our world to be safe. As a result we feel separated and disconnected from life.

Having gone through the depths of the grieving process, we become more surrendered to what is. There is a new openness with more wisdom and less judgment. Levine points out that, "Acceptance is not in the mind. It is in your heart. True acceptance comes from letting go of who you thought you were, opening to the vast connectedness and the universal compassion that lies just beneath the grasping at separate thoughts of a separate self, opening right now to the great unknown moment, unfolding as it will instant to instant."[17] Mary shares how surrender emerged from her process of facing her pain and suffering.

When my son died there was nowhere that my mind could go to escape the pain. Feelings that I had previously been able to suppress were constantly with me. The fact that I had other children was comforting, but I was attached to each of them. The loss of one left a gaping hole in my heart. My life felt out of control and all I could do from moment-to-moment was surrender.

In this process there is often a deepening of our spiritual awareness as we become less attached to others, to the objects in our lives, and to how things turn out. As our expectations ease, we start to see grief as a personally transforming experience. As we relax into the process, we find ourselves more willing to let go of needing things to remain the same. Through grief we learn to let go of how we want or expect life to be. Learning how to love without clinging is a very difficult but essential step in accepting the spiritual opportunity offered by life.

Self-Transformation

Being that the time of grieving is a spiritually auspicious time, the grieving process doesn't always end with acceptance. Anytime we experience a change, we also change. When we open ourselves to that change, and use it as a vehicle for personal and spiritual growth, we become transformed.[18] The process of self-transformation was a key part of Mary's process.

My son's death was the most traumatic experience of my life. At the same time, it broke me open, and I went to heights in my spiritual process that I could never have reached without that experience. I could relate to what Stephen Levine said to a woman whose son had died, "You may even have moments of ecstasy, because on another level you are in touch with the great mystery of life and something in you knows it and is ecstatic to be facing the truth."[19]

Opening to grief allows us to come back to ourselves, to become more in touch with our true nature. We respond to life with a more expanded and balanced view having been so profoundly affected. We become more sensitive and spontaneous in our lives. Compassion and wisdom, rather than fear and contraction, become the norm.

Many of the world's scriptures speak of a treasure within much like the story that begins this book. In the *Katha Upanishad*, it is written that, "One looks outward, not within himself. The wise man, while seeking immortality, introspectively beheld the Soul face-to-face."[20]

In the Sermon on the Mount in Matthew 6:19-21, Christ tells his disciples, "Don't store up treasures here on earth where they can erode away. Store them in heaven where they will never lose their value. If your profits are in heaven, your heart will be there too."[21]

Swami Rama says that, "This treasure is hidden within, buried under layers of ego, desires, emotions, habits, and other imbedded thought patterns. Peeling off the layers of imbedded thought patterns is not so easy. Shankara said that a treasure doesn't come out when you call it. It must be hunted for and dug up. All that is heaped over the buried treasure must be removed."[22]

This treasure is eternal—*atman,* the soul, the pure Self, our true identity—that which Genesis 1:26 claims is in the image and likeness of God,[23] the diamond that is the reflection of our true nature. We have to dig through the pain of grief, and all that arises in this process, in order to discover the treasure buried deep within.

Chapter 5

The Passage Through Grief

If you love the life that clings to the body, then you grieve when the body dies. Avoid this grief by truly loving the Self, for there is no pain of parting from this life behind all life.
Muruganar
Homage to the Presence of Sri Ramana

Opening to the energy and power of one's feelings can be challenging. When the feelings are especially painful, we just want to run the other way. Yet, this opening is essential in the process of inner discovery.[1] Judy, whose mother had recently died, told us how much she was learning about herself and the patterns of her mind. "I tried to take the straight path through grief but instead I found myself on a country road with all the twists and turns and found it to be much more interesting and beautiful."

This journey to find the treasure within can take many surprising turns. When we experience a heart-wrenching loss, the process we go through in order to let go of our attachment involves surrendering our sense of security in the world without having as yet reached the sacred within. How do we find that sense of non-attachment when our world is turned upside down, and all that we want to do is scream at the injustice of it all?

WORKING WITH GRIEF

We now turn to particular methods or means that can be used to navigate these narrow straits in our journey. Each of these represent a different way to help the person move through the intensity of the grieving process.

Journaling

Keeping a journal of our inner experiences can be beneficial, especially when the grief is severe. In this state, we want to tell our story over and over again. It is nature's way of helping us to realize, and slowly integrate, the loss. The journal can become our best friend when we don't wish to talk with anyone, or when no one wants to listen any longer because we have told the same story so many times before.

The journal can also serve as a reference point when, weeks or months down the road, the shock wears off, and it seems as if there has been no movement beyond the initial painful reaction to the loss. During these times, we can look back in our journal and realize that we really have progressed, even though it may still feel as if the loss had just occurred.

As we begin to feel the intensity of our feelings, the journal becomes a forum to express and, at times, resolve our emotional disturbances. When anger arises, for example, and our reactions feel out of control, the very act of writing down one's feelings helps to dissolve the reactivity, resolve the more immediate conflict, and bring awareness to the pain beneath the anger.

Perhaps most importantly, keeping a journal helps to bring unconscious patterns and emotions into conscious awareness. The time of intense grieving is a time that affects one's sense of self and how one views the world. It shakes our very being. As we bring awareness to the patterns of our minds that keep us defended, journal writing can facilitate a shift in these mental/emotional patterns by offering new insights and unblocking the barriers to transforming our lives.

Dreamwork

Dreams are a way used by the psyche to integrate the loss. By carefully investigating the nature and meaning of these dreams, we can facilitate this process of integration. Dreams are rich with symbolism and can be an important source for understanding the nature of our grief, and for showing us our progression in the grieving process. Dreams can also be comforting when a person we love reveals important information or simply comes to us in the dream, as in Mary's experience.

After Ted died, I had a series of vivid dreams of him that I recorded in my journal and then worked on in order to understand their deeper meaning.

In the first dream, he rocked me back and forth in a playful way as he hugged me. He then suddenly backed away, wondering what was wrong. I did not want to tell him that he had died. In dream after dream, I was teaching him about his death and about life after death. It was as though he was still alive. A month later, I dreamt that my family was having a buffet dinner. I turned around to see that Ted had come back and had taken a plate to have dinner with us. I told him that he could not stay and had to leave. It was one of the hardest things that I had ever done even though it was only a dream. When I awakened, I was sobbing. I was one step closer to letting go of him.

Dreams can be elusive and are often difficult to remember. The more you honor your dreams, however, the more you remember them. By having a pad and pencil with a small light by your bed, you can record your dreams immediately when you awaken. Read over what you have written and then underline the images. See what you associate with each image. Jung referred to this technique as "association."[2] For example, if there is a car in your dream, you would ask yourself, "What do I think of when I see a car?" Or, you may simply describe the image, a technique Jung referred to as "amplification."

When people appear in your dreams, ask yourself what characteristics each person has. After writing about each of the images, and connecting the dream with what is transpiring in your daily life, the meaning of the dream will gradually unfold. Jung would say that the way to know that your particular interpretation was opening you to a deeper truth was by having an "ah ha" experience. Robert Johnson in *Inner Work*[3] and Swami Radha in *Realities of the Dreaming Mind*[4] also offer ways to identify the message that may be contained in the dream.

At other times, dreams speak to us directly regarding difficult issues. Some of Mary's dreams have addressed issues involving death and dying.

I recall a time when I was intimately exploring my beliefs, thoughts, and feelings regarding death. I had two dreams at that time that I found instrumental in this process. In the first dream, I enter a large building where many people have been sitting for years as though asleep. Sitting next to each individual were twenty-five to fifty clones of that individual. Each clone is making a different repetitive movement as though stuck in that movement. I see Elisabeth Kubler-Ross sleeping on the ground in the midst of all of them muttering a word in her sleep. I am told that she holds the key to each person being whole and waking up. I kneel close to her so that I can hear what she is saying. She keeps repeating the word *moksha* (a Sanskrit word for spiritual freedom or liberation).

In the second dream, I see someone sitting on the ground watching me. He is very powerful and could kill me instantly if he wished. I am not afraid of him. In fact, I find it challenging to know him. I point my finger at him, and see my energy envelop him. I see another, at a distance behind him, and then another and then yet others, one at a time, until five appear. They are like figures of death. One has a large skeleton head with a small body. He dies as I'm watching. As I look at his face carefully, others gather around him. Even though they see him as ugly, in my eyes, he is beautiful.

The first dream shows how we are not whole within ourselves, but have parts and processes that are in some ways split off. Each clone represents a part of ourselves that has become separated and acts out of unconscious patterning, that defends us from the pain we, for whatever reason, will not look at. Swami Rama claims that the fear of death is the basis of all fear.[5] This truth, in the dream, is represented by Elisabeth Kubler-Ross, the woman who did so much in bringing awareness to the dying process.

When we are no longer afraid of death, as in the second dream, we then realize on a deeper level that there is no need to defend ourselves from the natural processes of life. We can then live life with more awareness. We become more willing to go into the depths of ourselves and see this process as an adventure, rather than as an entering into a dreadful dungeon that we must somehow, in some way, avoid.

Physical Well-Being and Breathing Exercise

Since our bodies are vehicles for spirit, it is important that they be healthy when taking on the additional stress that grieving brings. Since we lack motivation during this time, we often neglect the care of our bodies. Eating and sleeping disturbances, fatigue, and various ailments are all too common when grieving. With the added stress on our bodies, we are more susceptible to illness. Maintaining proper nutrition can be difficult in that we usually do not feel motivated to prepare our own meals, often resorting to so-called "junk foods" that are notoriously heavy in carbohydrates and sugar. It is important to eat a balanced diet. Limiting or eliminating caffeine, nicotine, refined sugar, alcohol, and chemical additives also reduces stress-related symptoms and is helpful in preventing further health problems.

When it is difficult to sleep at night, short naps can reduce the tension often created by the lack of sleep. Or, when one's working schedule does not allow for naps, periodic stretching and short meditations done throughout the day can help to bring one back to center. Daily exercise increases flexibility as well as muscle tone and strength, and stimulates the production of endorphins, thus helping us to feel brighter and more energized. Finding an exercise that we enjoy, such as swimming, walking, bicycling, or one of the movement practices such as hatha yoga or T'ai Chi, will increase the likelihood that we will continue to exercise on a regular basis.

How we breathe is something that most of us do not usually attend to. We do not realize that our breath is both a regulator and indicator of one's level of stress, and that most individuals have developed the tension-inducing habit of breathing in a purely thoracic fashion. The following diaphragmatic breathing exercise, practiced for twenty minutes a day for twelve weeks, leads to a slower breathing rate, lower heart rate, and increased efficiency of oxygen exchange, thus quieting the mind and helping to lower our anxiety and emotional reactivity.[6]

Relaxation and diaphragmatic breathing exercise

Lying down on your back with your feet slightly apart and your hands at your sides, palms up, breathe gently through your nostrils so that your abdomen rises and falls, while your chest stays relatively still. Breathe diaphragmatically, and breathe as smoothly and as evenly as you can. And relax, from the top of your head to the tips of your toes. Relax your toes and your feet. Relax your ankles. Relax your calves and your knees. Relax your thighs. Breathing gently, relax your pelvic region, your hip joints, your genital area, and your buttocks. Relax the small of your back, and relax your abdomen. Relax your chest, your shoulders, and your shoulder blades. With smooth, even breathing, relax your upper arms, your elbows, your lower arms, your wrists, your hands, and your fingers. Let yourself be still. Relax your neck muscles. Relax your face, your forehead, eyebrows, and eyes. Relax your cheeks, your lips, your tongue, and your jaw. Let your whole body be heavy. Check your body for tension, and if you find any, just let it go. Let it drain away, as you begin to withdraw your attention inwards. Leave the world out there and go inside. Feel your breath, down into your lungs, and continue breathing so that your tummy rises and falls with a gentle movement of your diaphragm. A helpful image is of an ocean wave in the open sea—the heaving sea just rises and falls but never stops. Breathe like the heaving sea, so that your inhalation slowly becomes your exhalation, and your exhalation slowly becomes your inhalation, without a pause. As you breathe, you may notice a number of pauses and hesitations in your breathing. Do your best to smooth out your breath, and breathe as smoothly and as evenly as you can. Remember to stay relaxed. Feel your mind relaxing. As you follow the gentle rise and fall of your breath, continue with the practice in this way for as long as you wish. And, when you feel ready, slowly bring your awareness back into your body. Carefully move your limbs once again, and gently open your eyes. Return to a seated position.

To maintain or maximize our health and create optimal wellness is difficult under more everyday circumstances, but is especially challenging during the grieving process. In *The Wellness Tree,* Justin O'Brien offers a practical self-care model that can be especially helpful during these times. His approach is designed to transform ordinary health and ensuing decline into real possibilities for not only one's rejuvenation, but also for sensitizing and deepening one's spiritual inclinations. He tells us, "Promoting optimal wellness means the continuing self-realization of the human potential in body, mind, and spirit. It is the process of actualizing a body that is strong, fit, and pleasurable; a mind that is curious, balanced, and reflective and that operates with an ease towards other beings; a spirit that is constantly and mutually self-enriching in its relationships with the cosmos."[7] Remaining aware of this perspective when we are grieving helps guide us through the grief process and minimizes the chance that we will become stuck or lost in our grief.

Creative Expression

Our creativity can be expressed through many different forms including painting, poetry, writing, collage, dance, playing a musical instrument, or singing. True creativity comes from the depths of our being, and involves expressing whatever emerges. During the grieving process, any of these or other forms of expression can release the intensity of the emotional pain that we are experiencing as a result of the loss. Mary describes how she used one of these forms.

After my son's death when my emotions were particularly intense, such as during holidays, his birthday, or the anniversary of his death, or at other times when I was feeling "stuck" in the pain of my grief, I would make a collage. In this creative process, insights would come, the energy would shift, and I once again felt in the flow of life.

In collage work, one allows the images to come forward from the unconscious by being aware of the sensations in one's body when looking at magazine pictures or photographs. If one feels moved by, or simply finds oneself dwelling on, a particular picture, put the picture aside. Repeat this process as many times as necessary until you feel finished and then, using your intuition as a guide, first arrange and then paste the pictures onto a large piece of paper. When done, sit with your completed collage, exploring and experiencing any insights that may come forward.

The Sacredness of Ritual

Rituals have been used throughout time by many different cultures and religious traditions. They help communicate and express our emotions symbolically in a way that is difficult or impossible to express in other ways. They touch a core place in us and often have a cathartic effect.

Two of the more important rituals involving death are the funeral and the memorial service. Both of these can be very therapeutic. A primary benefit of the funeral is that it confirms the reality of the death. We actually see the body without life, and have to make plans for the burial. If the body is cremated, the finality can be even more pronounced. Mary describes this experience of finality.

I was able to see Ted's body laid out for three days before the funeral, and as I viewed his body, I cried as his death slowly became more real. However, when the mortuary director closed the casket, it really struck me that this was it. He was gone.

Some people find it helpful to get involved in designing the funeral or memorial service in the way that they believe their loved one would have wanted, or in the way that nurtures them in the grieving process. Others find that their energy is so depleted that they are unable to be a part of the planning. Those of us who are able to participate often find this kind of planning conducive to feeling more finished or complete with the person we loved. Consider Mary's experience.

I was fortunate enough to participate in this process while others carried out the plans. My sister-in-law played the guitar and sang my son's favorite songs, Ted's friends and cousins carried the coffin, and my husband's uncle, who was a priest, presided over the service. Afterwards, many people participated by bringing food for the reception that followed.

Joanne, whose son Jerry had died, found it healing to have his memorial service in a funeral home with balloons and Teddy bears next to a picture album of their son for people to look at. They invited friends and relatives to tell their favorite story about him.

These rituals offer a way in which friends and relatives can grieve together, thereby providing support for one another. In addition, rituals provide an opportunity for saying good-bye, to say "I love you" or "I miss you," and for sharing past experiences of the loved one.

In *Who Dies?* Stephen Levine writes, "A funeral is an opportunity to acknowledge the love we have shared, as well as to remember the departed to continue on their journey without clinging to the life left behind. It is a ritual that encourages the heart to open its grief as well as to trust in what exists beyond the senses. The funeral is a skillful means to remind the departed as well as those left that they are not simply a body."[8]

Other kinds of rituals are also important. During the holidays, birthdays, and anniversaries, when grief is so poignant, one can create a ritual that honors the loved one and helps to integrate the intense feelings that are arising. It can be a candle flame, flowers at the gravesite, a special ornament in remembrance, or a few meaningful words at the holiday meal. Rituals can also be helpful when there are unresolved issues involving the person who died or as a closing ceremony when the grieving process feels finished. Mary relates such an incident.

Jamie was five years old when her parents died in an automobile accident. Now, after two years of grieving the loss, her parents' death was no longer the main focus of her life. She was able to continue without the deep sadness that kept her trapped in the past. We went to the beach where she wrote her mom a note. She then put her message in a helium balloon and released it. After we watched in silence as the balloon disappeared into the clouds, she turned to me and said, "Do you think mommy got it?"

Writing a letter or a poem and then reading it at the gravesite, talking to a picture of the deceased, planting a tree where the accident occurred, or any other ritual that expresses how it is for you, or represents your life with that individual, can be a catalyst that helps to bring closure to this chapter in your life. It is difficult, however, to know what effect any particular ritual will have. The grieving process unfolds at different rates in different ways for different people at different times.

Inner Awareness Through Imagery

Whenever we are experiencing emotional or physical pain, rather than succumbing to the pain and becoming lost in it, we can move through it, or at least lessen the intensity of the pain, by paying attention to the sensations that arise in our bodies. A method using imagery that we have found especially sensitive to revealing and dissipating the physical, bodily manifestations of grief is one inspired by A.H.Almaas.[9]

Based on Almaas' discussions of self-observation and spiritual development, we offer the following adaptation of his work that is designed to help us facilitate our journey through the pain. This exercise can help us to experience and integrate what we are feeling, especially at times when we are feeling lost in or overwhelmed by our grief and its related emotions.

Symbolic Imagery Exercise

Allow the energy to arise in your body, and describe it to yourself as though it were an object. Give it a shape, a color, a size. Investigate the object, and feel its texture in your mind's eye. Is it soft, prickly, hard, cold, hot, wet, or smooth? Notice how you feel about it. Are you afraid of this object? Are you feeling angry that it is there? Do you see it as beautiful or ugly? Do you have compassion for it? Whatever your feelings, just notice them. Don't judge what is arising. Ask the image what it wants and see what emerges. A surprising thought may appear or the image may change.

Working with the image by asking it various questions, and talking with it and observing what emerges, tends to transform the energy. The painful intensity often lessens, and, in some cases, the energy actually changes, or even dissolves completely.

DEEPENING THE EXPERIENCE OF THE SACRED

Having faced and integrated the painful issues that initially blocked our path, the following ways can deepen our understanding of the sacred dimensions that await our attention within.

Being and Presence

Many of us identify with our minds and bodies much of the time. By mind we are referring to that field of energy that includes our thoughts, emotions, and perceptions, as well as the material stored in our unconscious. Identifying with the mind and its contents keeps us separate, as when we lock onto concepts, judgments, and beliefs, thus blocking our authenticity and spontaneity. Instead of being an instrument, or a bridge between the outer and inner worlds, we often let the mind dominate us. As a result, our minds become a detriment to our well-being rather than being a means to attaining conscious awareness. This results in discontent.

John Welwood, in *Journey of the Heart*, reflects on these issues. "In

Western society, we are constantly encouraged to take our minds away from the present. We learn to occupy ourselves desperately; to do several things simultaneously. We feel best when busy, with our minds split off in different directions. Our conversation is carefully edited before it goes out onto the air. It is screened for social acceptability. 'How will what I say influence the way others see me?' Such activity is more concerned with becoming somebody rather than being someone. We learn to package ourselves, to protect certain kinds of images, rather than simply to be."[10]

The key seems to be, while resisting the mind's inclination to go out and become entangled in the things and events of the world, to return one's focus to the power and value of simply being. When we bring conscious awareness to the moment without judgment, we are less likely to react to our emotions, project them onto others, or store them in our bodies. We need the patience and discipline to stay present in the now until the Now becomes the ground. By staying present in the moment, we are less likely to identify with our body-mind and are more likely to open to a deeper more intuitive way of being.

As we become aware of the silence behind the thoughts and the patterns of our minds, we begin to feel a profound stillness. In the Bible, Psalm 46:10 states, "Be still and know that I am God."[11] This deep inner stillness is the ground of what we refer to as presence. Presence is not a quality of personality, such as charisma, but is, rather, rooted in our spiritual essence.

History has identified many individuals whose very being evoked peace, joy, and love, as well as feelings of inspiration, awe, and great respect, in those fortunate enough to have experienced the consciousness-transforming power of their presence. The names of Christ, Moses, Krishna, Buddha, Mohammed, and other revered spiritual figures have resonated in our hearts and minds down through the ages. This profound stillness lies within each of us. It awaits our recognition.

With practice, our sense of stillness deepens and we feel more alert, aware, and connected to our divine Self. With this communion with all-pervading consciousness that permeates all of life, the identification with our own essence becomes stronger. We recognize this within ourselves when we are willing to be present with what is in the moment. The deeper one's identification with essence, the more powerful one's presence.

Eckart Tolle says, "Give attention to the present, to your behavior, to your reactions, moods, thoughts, emotions, fears, and desires as they occur in the present. *There's* the past in you. If you can be present enough to watch all those things, not critically or analytically but non-judgmentally, then you are dealing with the past and dissolving it through the power of your presence. You cannot find yourself by going into the past. You find yourself by coming into the present."[12]

The following exercise is designed to help one to experience this inner essence.

Exercise in Being with the Present

Experience the moment. Start by closing your eyes and observing the thoughts in your mind and the sensations in your body without judging or labeling them. Notice any contractions. Feel your body breathing. Listen to the sounds around you, as you take the sounds within. You may hear the birds singing, the ticking of the clock, or the sound of flowing water. Without judging, take it all in. If you find yourself judging or ruminating, just bring yourself back to the present moment and observe your breath. Listen to the silence. Feel the stillness in the silence that gives birth to the thoughts and sounds in your mind, and the sensations in your body. Feel the stillness behind the form. If tears come, just allow them to flow without analyzing or obsessing about the content. See if the contractions are starting to ease. Become aware of any joy that may be arising, as you feel your body relaxing and your mind quieting. Retain this awareness as you gently open your eyes and your attention returns to the world around you. Remember to remain in the moment on all levels of your being as you go on with your day.

When we practice stillness or being here now, we are gradually able to find that deeper consciousness, that sacred place where love, joy, and peace reside.

Contemplation and Prayer

Contemplation and prayer refer to practices in which one can open to the deeper, sacred dimensions of one's being. Each practice, in its own way, represents a dialogue, or the opportunity for a dialogue, between one's conscious ego-self and one's essence or soul, between the drop and the ocean beyond. For this to occur, a certain degree of detachment and emotional nonreactivity with regard to the outer world is essential so that the mind can remain primarily inwardly attuned.

Contemplation, in its simplest and purest form, refers to focusing the mind on a single source of spiritual inspiration and importance. One might, for example, mentally reflect upon or contemplate the meaning of a particular scripture, the picture of a great spiritual master, the beauty of a sunset, or the power of a piece of music to transform one's level of consciousness or awareness.

In any event, the first step is to turn your attention inward, freeing yourself from everyday concerns, and being committed to approaching any thoughts and feelings that arise with gentle compassion. Prayer also involves a turning within, but, unlike contemplation *per se,* one actively attempts to converse directly with God or the Divine Source. This prayerful contact often takes the form of a request, either to help one find the love, wisdom, and strength within oneself to deal with some challenge or difficulty in life, or for God to actually intercede in order to remedy the difficulty directly, as when we pray for divine assistance or intervention.

As part of his efforts to renew the contemplative tradition in Christianity, Thomas Keating, a Christian monk, addresses the nature of contemplative prayer as, "the opening of mind and heart—of our whole being—to God, the Ultimate Mystery, beyond thoughts, words, and emotions ... who we know is within us."[13] He describes contemplative prayer as "a process of interior transformation" where God initiates an inner conversation with us that, if we consent, may ultimately lead us to union with God.[14]

Addressing contemplation in a similar way, Rajmani Tigunait writes, "Try to feel what you are thinking. This is a dialogue between the unawakened and wakened soul within you. You are both orator and audience, teacher and student, counselor and client. You are both subject and object. As the thoughts flow and emotions are evoked, let them form themselves as tears or smiles; let them manifest silently or verbally; let them stir your entire being. Let the deepest core of your heart be touched by these contemplative thoughts."[15]

Concentration and Meditation

Meditation has been suggested, over thousands of years in different forms in different cultures, as a practical method for working with both the contents of and one's primary identification with the mind in order to know the eternal, unchanging soul or sacred Self as one's true and deepest nature. The meditative process is, in this way, a process of true self-transformation.[16]

The practice of meditation is most often preceded by concentration. As a process, concentration involves giving the mind one thing to focus on such as a word, a set of syllables (for example, a mantra), or phrase (for example, the Jesus Prayer) that one repeats silently in one's mind, or a visual image such as a candle flame or picture. Although a subtle and difficult art to master, practicing concentration is not a tedious task. In fact, the experience of sustained concentration is often reported to be pleasant and satisfying.

As one practices concentration in a systematic fashion, two things begin to occur with increasing frequency and intensity. First, the general content and noise level of the mind is reduced as the mind becomes quieter during the practice. Second, in the context of this deepening stillness, one begins a natural process of watching or witnessing the mind's thoughts and emotions from a place of peaceful non-attachment, slowly breaking one's identification with the mind and its contents. With continued practice and awareness, one eventually acquires the ability to bring one's mind to one-pointedness or pure focus at will. This ability to focus the mind is a prerequisite for true meditative experience as the effortless flow of timeless awareness. It is in the direct experience of this content-less flow that one's true Self or soul nature is revealed.[17]

A meditation can be as simple as closing our eyes, sitting with our head, neck, and spine straight, and focusing on the smooth, even flow of our breath. Beginning with an extensive relaxation exercise designed to relax our body systematically from head to toe, we can then relax our mind by observing any thoughts or feelings that arise, and letting them go as we bring our wandering attention back to the breath. A practiced pattern of smooth, even diaphragmatic breathing quiets the breath and mind so that one can access even deeper states of meditative stillness.

In his book, *Meditation and the Art of Dying,* Swami Veda explores a more specific role that meditation plays in the process of self-transformation and spiritual development.[18] As meditation progresses, and one becomes better able to observe the mind's contents from a detached inner place, identifying more deeply with this impartial observer, three things begin to happen. First, one grieves less over the loss of the physical body, second, one's ego-identification begins to break-up, and, third, ego loses its need to control. Ego identity and ego dependency literally begin to die. In this sense, meditation is truly a dying practice. If one practices dying daily in this way, then there will be a greater familiarity with the process, and, thereby, less fear of and resistance to dying when it is one's time to die.

Chapter 6

Moving Toward the Sacred

Among all the passions inflicted from without, death holds the first place.
Consequently, when a person conquers death and things directed to death, this is
most perfect.   Thomas Aquinas
Summa Theologica

Having addressed the relationship among living, dying, and grieving
in Chapter 1, and having described in some detail the processes of
dying and grieving in Chapters 2 through 5, we now turn to the implications
of these discussions. As a person faces his or her mortality directly, basic
questions arise. What is life on earth really about? What is the meaning
of life? What is the purpose of having a mind and body? What is the soul?
Does the soul animate the body/mind? What keeps us from realizing our
soul-nature? It seems that our identification with and attachment to the
persons and things of the world keep us distracted at best and, most often,
ignorant of our true identity as the conscious, eternal, unchanging soul or
spiritual Self. This chapter begins with a closer look at the nature, function,
and power of attachment, so that we might better understand how we
become entangled in the web of life. This entanglement is in the very fabric
of the fear of death.

THE ANATOMY OF ATTACHMENT

The importance of letting go of what we are attached to is given special
emphasis in a number of spiritual systems and traditions. The twelve-step

program of Alcoholics Anonymous, for example, offers the aphorism "Let go, let God," the heartfelt advice being to surrender to a greater reality. As mentioned earlier, the Christian tradition emphasizes the importance of ego surrender while the yoga tradition regards not being attached to the outcome of your actions as a key to spiritual realization. As another example, Buddhism stresses the importance of realizing the impermanence of all things in the process of becoming enlightened.[1] Basing one's happiness on that which is impermanent, that is, becoming attached, leads directly to suffering.

Attachment is so much a part of our lives, it usually works outside of our awareness. Even when recognized, it is difficult to comprehend. What is this phenomenon that we have come to call attachment? An accepted understanding is that it refers to how our minds anchor us to other people and objects in our lives, and the dynamics that keep us there. We attach ourselves to others and to objects of the world out of fear that somehow we will lose them if we do not hold on. We are also afraid that we will not have what this person or thing means to us when we want or need it. People often think of love and attachment as being inseparable. Attachment, however, often reduces our capacity to truly love. In attachment, we are identified with the ego-self and its needs, wants, and preferences, whereas unselfish love comes from a deeper place within, reflecting a selfless state of being.

If grief is, indeed, the result whenever someone or something that we have become attached to dies or simply changes, then understanding the process of attachment seems essential if we are to live our lives free from pain and suffering. If attachment becomes an unconscious habit of mind, grief will become chronic since everything in life changes.

In the same way that moving through the grieving process has a recognized pattern, there is also a process we go through when we become attached to people, places, objects, ideas, situations, and relationships. What happens to us? How do we become attached? What is it within us that is afraid and wants to cling to this world, when we know in the depths of our being that the world will not give us lasting satisfaction? We know we can't take anything with us when we die! People often speak with insight when they say things such as, "When I meditate, I feel so peaceful," or, "When I follow the truth within myself, I feel more joyful and loving." Yet, we habitually gravitate to mundane things of the world in search of satisfaction.

Taking on a human body and coming into this material world, we feel separate from the Divine. Our senses tend to focus outward on what we see, hear, taste, touch, and smell. We find ourselves being so dependent on the world and what it has to offer that we lose touch with the truth of who we are. In addition, we see the world in a dualistic way. In an unconsciously conditioned way, we see things in terms of right-wrong, good-bad, moral-immoral, light-dark, fair-unfair, masculine-feminine, approval-disapproval, intelligent-unintelligent, and a host of other polarities or opposites. We tend to forget that there is one essential thread shared by all that is. If we realized the truth of this shared essence in our day-to-day experience, that is, if we actually experienced this place where we are all one, then there would be no perceived separateness. Attachment, therefore, would have no ground in which to grow. There would be no "other" in our universe and, therefore, nothing outside of ourselves to possess.

Most of us, however, are not taught to go within to find that love that so many of us hunger for, so we look for it outside of ourselves. When we see someone that we are attracted to and in whose presence we feel love, for instance, we want to nurture that love, but soon we fear that it will be lost. As a result, we obsess about and, consciously or unconsciously, want to possess and control that person who we mistakenly believe is our connection to those loving feelings. The love, joy, and feelings of expansion become fear, jealousy, and feelings of contraction.

Coming into this world as infants, we discover that in order to get our needs met, we must rely on the adults in our lives. Mixed with our love for them, we become bound and want to please them. Gradually we learn to individuate as we grow into adulthood, our ego helping us to separate from others. It is when we become solely identified with this ego that the problems arise.

When we see a sunset we are often in awe, and, then, when the sky changes, we go on with our lives. When we get a new job, buy a new car, or look forward to the future, however, we enjoy our experience at first but often become fearful of what will happen in the future. Will my job provide enough money? Will my car get stolen? Will my child be successful? Will I lose my beauty as I age? Rather than just enjoying the experience, we become afraid of losing what we have or not getting what we want. We even suffer when we get what we want, because all things decay or dissolve over time and we resist their natural change. We forget that everyone and everything is on loan. We forget to live in the now.

A central thread in the fabric of attachment is looking outside, rather than within, for who we are and what we need. As long as we are looking outside of ourselves for gratification we feel incomplete.

Joan's husband died just five years after they were married. She described the process of her relationship with him.

After Frank died, I began to realize how attached I was to him, how I lost myself in him and depended on him to make me whole. It wasn't like that at first. I remember when we first met. I had been alone for several years. I felt independent and confident in who I was. I remember Frank telling me he liked that in me. I so enjoyed being with him. When we weren't together, I still felt present and involved in life. I felt a love for everybody, a love for life itself. We married soon after we met. As time passed, I wanted to be with him more and more, missing him when he wasn't around. I found myself defining myself through him and felt lost without him. I started to worry about his heart condition, a condition that he had lived with all of his life, afraid that he would die. I also found myself feeling jealous when other women would flirt with him. We started arguing and I didn't like how I was or what was happening to our relationship. I felt miserable with him, yet didn't want to let him go. Life just wasn't satisfying to me any longer. I felt like I still loved him, but it was tainted by my need for him. Life has been hard these past two years since Frank's death. I felt devastated when he first died and didn't think I could live without him. Since his death, I have gradually become more aware of how intertwined our lives had been and how much I had depended on him to complete me.

Even though modern life offers many comforts, people are often not content. Instead of simply enjoying the people and things of this world, we have a tendency to become identified and attached. We cling to them, own them, and fear losing them. We become tangled in our own expectations, beliefs, defense mechanisms, resentments, and preconceived notions. All of these are, in one way or another, tied to attachment and keep us from living a full and meaningful life.

The roots of our attachments run deep. The notion that we need things in the world in order to feel worthy and complete in ourselves is passed down from generation to generation. Most of us observed this in our parents, internalized this pattern, and modeled it for our children. When we change these patterns in our minds, however, we can break the chain and, thereby, benefit all of those who follow.

When we speak of attachment, we are referring to aversion as well as attraction. Aversion is similar to attraction in that the object of our aversion occupies our minds. When we dislike or fear someone or something, our minds get caught, and our time and energy is spent in anger, resentment, fear, worry, or avoidance in our attempt to push away or rid ourselves of the discomfort.

Swami Muktananda once said, "The wise man gets angry and is joyful the next moment. The fool gets angry and takes it to his grave." The wise man experiences anger and then quickly returns to joyfulness once the wave of anger has passed. His identity with the true Self is so strong that he quickly returns to his basic nature after being disturbed. Yet, how many times do we "take things to our grave" and, if not for a lifetime, hold on to negative feelings for minutes, hours, days, months, or years? It is as if our minds have fingers, grab the pain, and won't let go.

There are degrees of attachment, all the way from the subtle clinging involved when we give a gift to someone because we want them to like us or to feel some sense of obligation, to becoming obsessed with or addicted to relationships, drugs, gambling, food, money, sex, or power. All of these provide only temporary satisfaction. Regardless of the form or degree, we lose ourselves in attachment. Our egos may feel safe, at least for the time being, but a deeper part of us feels deadened.

We give up our freedom when we become attached or addicted, in both obvious and, sometimes, very subtle ways. Consider this example offered by Swami Veda. "Imagine that you have become addicted to eating chocolate cake. You have struggled with your addiction and, after years of spiritual practice and bringing awareness to your craving, you now believe that you are once again free. If, however, you say to yourself, 'I can now walk by the refrigerator and not open the door and eat the chocolate cake,' you are still caught! Your eating behavior may have changed, but your mind still leaps onto the chocolate cake when you walk by the refrigerator."[2] True freedom occurs when the mind is in the moment and neither goes toward nor moves away from anyone or anything.

All attachments involve fear, whether we fear losing that which we are attracted to, or facing that which we are averse to. As a result, we attempt to control the environment, other people, situations, as well as our own thoughts and behaviors in order to minimize the loss or maximize our pleasure and sense of security.

Attachment tends to separate us, whereas simply enjoying what we have in the moment often provides a sense of connectedness and continuity. There is a rhythm to life. A heartbeat, the ocean waves, the rising and setting of the sun, are all a part of that melody. When we are present in the moment and listen to the stillness of our being, we too feel this rhythm.

Whenever we talk about attachment, we are talking about our identification with someone or something. Our desire to possess or our inclination to obsess comes from our fear. Whenever we resist the change in someone or something that we hold dear, our reaction is often visceral. This reaction has its roots in our fear of death. Once again, reflecting on the fear of death deepens our understanding and acceptance.

In this regard, consider the following words of Christina Grof. "If we accept that someday our physical bodies will die, then at a certain point we realize we will not be able to hold on to our possessions, roles, or relationships forever. Someday we will leave this earth and all that we have identified with. Realizing all this can be devastating for someone who is attached to his or her identity as a parent, mate, landowner, socialite, or jobholder. Individuals who have put a great deal of time, effort, and money into their professional image, their athletic achievements, or their material possessions, often focus so intently on their goals that they lose sight of the fact that it is all temporary. The fear of death and our unwillingness to acknowledge and accept it is often a motivating factor in our attachments and addictions. If we are already uneasy because our life involves change, the fact that someday our lives will end is the utmost lesson in the transitory nature of existence."[3]

Swami Rama tells us, "Over the course of a lifetime of needing, having, and clinging, the fear of death grows and hovers, creating a spiral of more need, greater fear, and inescapable pain. In this way life cannot be lived effectively and is merely squandered. Death is feared, denied, and pushed as far away from consciousness as possible instead of being accepted as a natural and inevitable part of human experience. Thus, no one is prepared for death. This fear of death is the reason for the insatiable need for more things, ever new relationships, material comforts, endless entertainment, and the excessive use of alcohol and drugs. All of these keep the reality of death in the distance. They are the tools of denial."[4,5]

AN EXERCISE ON ATTACHMENT

The following exercise offers a simple way to become aware of our attachments and how these attachments might keep us from feeling fully present with what is in our lives. This exercise first explores how you know when you are attached.

Complete the following sentence with as many responses as come to mind. I am attached when:

Now turn your attention to how you feel when you are open to life and your experience. Complete the following sentence with as many responses as come to mind. I am alive when:

What follows are a list of Mary's personal responses to this exercise. We offer these, not as a complete list, but as examples of how the mind can become bound by what we perceive to be outside of ourselves, and how we feel when we extricate our mind from these ties.

I am attached when:

> I want to manipulate the person or situation in order to get my way, rather than going with the flow of what is.
> I habitually do something rather than coming from an awareness in the present.
> I look outside of myself for my security.
> I lose who I am, and find some thing or some person more important or more valuable than myself.
> I feel restless inside because I want something and am not getting it, or it is not going the way I expect or want it to go.

I feel afraid, sad, lonely, jealous, angry, bored, or embarrassed.

I feel bothered by someone who does or says something I don't agree with.

I give to another while expecting approval or something else in return.

I feel that there isn't enough time, money, love, or energy.

I feel that I am not enough.

I am alive when:

I can be with what is, and simply learn from it, enjoy it, and share it.

I feel satisfied and grateful about life, and good about who I am.

I feel a spacious and centered love for myself and others.

I open and trust the flow of life.

I feel more fully engaged with life.

I feel the awe and perfection of what is.

I feel like I have enough and I am enough.

I feel an internal freedom.

I can move easily from one emotion to another, not caught or bound by any of them.

Our attachments keep us from participating fully in life. By yearning for something in the future or being discontent with something in the past, we lose our experience of the present.

MOVING BEYOND ATTACHMENT, LOSS, AND GRIEF

By opening to the depths of our grief, we are developing a greater awareness of non-attachment. We are breaking up the patterns that keep us bound. Just as working with grief in this way can be a stepping-stone for deeper spiritual realization, there is a way to work with one's attachments that, ultimately, leads beyond.

"Be not attached to the fruits of your actions" means to play your part while realizing that the outcomes of your actions are not yours to control. Do what you can and leave the rest. It means not to act with the thought of gain or out of fear, but to simply do it because it is right as dictated by your intuitive sense or by the "still small voice" within, not because you are afraid of not having your needs met. Consider the words of Eckhart Tolle. "If there isn't joy, ease, and lightness in what we are doing, we are probably giving more attention to the results rather than being with what we are doing. We no longer pursue our goal with fear of failure nor paralyzed with inactivity when 'our deeper sense of self is derived from Being.'"[6]

Yet, we strongly identify with our ego-mind and abandon our true Self. In this way, we all know the feeling of abandonment. We all feel this loss, and when someone we love dies, it is a reminder of the greatest loss of all, the loss of our connection with the Spirit within. Journeying to the inner treasure leads to the stillness of the heart. This is the journey home.

When the mind is aware only of worldly existence, forgetting its spiritual ground, its choices are always colored by its reliance on outer conditions and things. It is, therefore, often quite difficult to discriminate between the mind's habitual clinging and what is really true behind the distortions created by our attachments to the pains and pleasures of this world. Reality is more clearly perceived when the ego steps back and no longer insists on having its way.

It is also difficult for the mind that is attached to this world to trust that when we truly surrender to that universal connection that lies beyond the mind, our existence will not be threatened. Addressing his disciples in Luke 12:24 and 12:27, Christ speaks to the power of surrender. "Look at the ravens. They don't plant or harvest or have barns to store away their food, and yet they get along all right, for God feeds them. Look at the lilies! They don't toil and spin. If God provides clothing for the flowers that are here today and gone tomorrow, don't you suppose that God will provide clothing for you?"[7]

In one of his many public lectures, Ram Dass once said, "The spiritual journey is like jumping out of a plane without a parachute. We are terrified of the fall until we realize that there is no ground."[8] When we are willing to surrender, everything in life changes. We see more clearly. We love more deeply. No longer worrying about survival or the outcomes of our actions, we relax into life.

The attached mind is inclined to go into the past or into the future. When we are present with what is in the moment, as the past arises and we bring our awareness to it without judgment, the pain dissolves. Likewise, by staying present in the moment, we are more likely to intuitively know how to plan for the future without being concerned about how things will turn out.

Non-attachment does not mean indifference. When we are not attached, we love more purely than when we identify with a person or object as the source of our happiness. We now have the freedom to follow what is true for us and to enjoy life as it unfolds. This love is a more expansive, inclusive love. The practice of non-attachment involves observing the mind's habit of dwelling on the past or future, and letting go by relaxing the grip of the mind's "fingers" from whatever it is currently grasping. By consistently being in the present moment, the need to control dissolves. A flower, for example, is not attached to what others think nor does it care about whether it lives or dies. Bugs crawl on it, bees gather its pollen, and people spray it with poison, yet the flower simply blooms and offers its fragrance. Regardless of circumstance, it simply is.

In the process of letting go of the fear, and thus the need to control, we fill the space with love and thus become more in tune with the flow of life. Spiritual practices such as contemplation, prayer, self-study, and meditation can facilitate a deeper awareness. This awareness allows us to express a love that radiates from our connection with the Divine.

SIX DOORWAYS TO THE SPIRITUAL REALM

When opening to our life experiences as spiritual opportunities, we quickly see how challenging this process can be. It is often very difficult to access and maintain the necessary meditative space around a given experience, especially if it's an emotionally charged one, or to discriminate between spiritual experience *per se* and the colorings that come from our conscious and unconscious judgments and reactions. This is not an easy task!

In an attempt to facilitate this discriminatory process, Aldous Huxley identified a significant number of elements or themes shared by the world's great spiritual traditions regarding the nature of transcendent/spiritual experience. Aldous Huxley did not seem particularly interested in the differences between any particular religions (these are often painfully clear), but, rather, in what all of these different traditions had in common. He collectively referred to these shared elements as the perennial philosophy.[9]

Toward this same end, Bishop William Swing[10] noted that discussions of dying and grieving, and how to be with one's mortality, hold a very real promise for healing the differences that exist among various religious traditions because everyone dies! His feeling was that deeper discussions of this kind that address core issues shared by everyone, regardless of their religion, age, nationality, or gender, will serve to break through the more arbitrary differences, relatively speaking, that people tend to identify with and hold onto so strongly.

In this same spirit, we have come to identify six interrelated, yet distinct, characteristics or qualities that each of us have experienced or demonstrated at one point or another in our daily lives. In other words, although not necessarily commonplace, they are known to us directly in our everyday experience. These are not offered as spiritual experiences in and of themselves, but, rather, as signposts or guidelines that point the way or serve as windows to the spiritual realm. They are each sparks that, if nurtured and fanned, feed the inner spiritual fire.

Confidence

This first characteristic may come as a surprise to some when presented as a means of recognizing or accessing one's sacred or spiritual nature. Recall the last time that you felt truly confident about someone or something in your life. You may remember a sense of literally "standing tall" and feeling an inner strength in this egoless state. In fact, one's posture often changes when just thinking of being confident in this way. The spine straightens; the shoulders go back; the head is held high; the chest opens.

There is no fear when one feels this deeper sense of confidence. There is a sense of completeness or sovereignty, an aloneness that is not lonely because there is no "other" in one's awareness. It is an intrapersonal experience that does not involve another. That is, we feel strong, not because we regard someone else as weak, but, rather, because we trust our experience. You know what's true for you! You are neither defensive nor closed to others' opinions. You are, in fact, open to changing your view if someone presents new information that transforms your experience. Yet, unless this transformation occurs, you continue to rest in the truth of your own experience, uninfluenced by the opinions, critical or otherwise, of others. An example follows from Ron's personal experience.

I recall seeing Mother Teresa in the early 1990s at a Catholic church in San Francisco. She was there as part of a religious ceremony receiving a number of young women into her order of nuns, the Sisters of Charity. When Mother Teresa walked past the aisle in which several of us were sitting, I felt a force emanating from her as if someone had literally put their hands on my chest and pushed me. Her presence was that powerful. I had the spontaneous experience that I was looking at someone who knew who she was, what her purpose in life was, and why she was there that day. She remained unaffected by what anyone thought of her, and radiated confidence in her very being. She wasn't cold. In fact, when she was with others, she was quite warm, engaging, and open. Their opinions and judgments of her and her work, however, had absolutely no effect on her presence, her sense of self, or, perhaps most importantly, her awareness of what was true and right for her.

Fearlessness

To live in this world without fear is an attractive idea to most everyone. The truth is, however, that most of us are afraid in some way, to some degree, most of the time, and often live our days with a general sense of tension or anxiety. When our minds are filled with fear, the more subtle realms of our intuitive and spiritual experiences are clouded over. When we do think of living without fear, we often conjure up an image of a fearless warrior, a Samurai-like figure, who enters combat without any concern or apprehension. This is not, however, what is meant by fearlessness in the present context.

Think of someone that you know, a friend or relative perhaps, who everyone phones whenever there is a crisis, someone who can always be counted on to offer calm, wise, balanced guidance while everyone else is reacting, often impulsively without sense or direction. There is something special about this person. They somehow remain unaffected by the panic of those around them. They don't get caught in the melodrama while everyone else is in an emergency frame of mind. They do not buy into the fear. They are like candles that do not flicker in the wind. Such persons call us out of our fears simply by being their fearless selves, and we like being called out of our fears because it feels real and true. An authentic life is a life lived without fear.

You may believe that fear is acceptable, even helpful in certain situations. Fear is not helpful! It is a deep, habitual, and learned response to a perceived threat that can be mastered and laid to rest. We were born without fear and can return, with intent and practice, to this natural way of being. Phil Nuernberger states, "No human being is born fearful. Rather, what is often mistaken for fear is an inborn, primitive drive for self-preservation; when we distort this powerful drive, we create fear."[11]

Imagine being confronted by an injured and angry grizzly bear while camping or walking in the woods. It is clear that you are in serious danger and may not, in fact, survive this encounter. The key question is, however, Are you more likely to survive if you react with panic, confusion, and a general fight or flight response, or if your thoughts and actions grow out of a calm, clear, and nonreactive state of mind? Our own feeling is the latter. It is a myth to believe that fear is necessary under such circumstances in order to survive.

Peacefulness

We have never met anyone who has said that he or she did not wish to have peace of mind. Yet, even though we all search for this inner quiet, we often speak and act in ways that evoke more uncertainty and reactivity in both ourselves and others. We often raise the noise level, stir the waters, and disturb the peace. It seems that the ego-self stays active in, as well as distracted by, the outside world in this way. It avoids what it fears by keeping itself from turning inward and experiencing whatever it is that covers the true Self, the treasure within. Ron shares his own experience of peace and deep stillness.

Many years ago, I was attending a week-long program on meditation and spirituality at a rural retreat center. About fifty of us were gathered in the dining hall one early evening for dinner and conversation. As is typical in such a setting, the noise level in the hall rose and fell as everyone ate their dinner and conversed with one another. Unbeknownst to us at the time, a spiritual teacher had entered the dining hall at one point and sat quietly meditating in one corner of the room.

Gradually, over the next five to ten minutes, a general sense of calm, peace, and quiet spontaneously came over everyone and everything. At first I noticed that the volume level of the many voices was, for no apparent reason, going down and down until eventually no one was speaking. Many of us, myself included, noticed an inner quiet emerging that finally led many of those seated in the hall to close their eyes and fall into a spontaneous meditative state.

The feeling was irresistible. I remember clearly that there had been a number of dogs barking and birds chirping outside the dining hall when this event first began. By the end, the dogs and birds had fallen into silence as well. An absolute, indescribable peace, stillness, and tranquility permeated everyone and everything both inside and outside the room.

At this point, the spiritual teacher stood up and began to speak with us about the experience we were having. He said that stillness is the natural state of the mind that reflects the ground of being and spiritual reality itself. Here is the peace that lies beyond our conceptual understanding.

Joyfulness

There is a deep joy that lies within us. This joy is a grateful joy—grateful for the spiritual opportunities that life offers us, and grateful for another day to learn more about ourselves, others, and the realm of spirit. This joy lies beyond the more obvious dimension of happy-sad. It does not fit easily, if at all, with the principles of pleasure and pain.

For example, we often enter a potentially painful situation knowing that this is something we need to face, master, and, thereby, overcome. Although the task or situation may be very difficult, we welcome the challenge, and will even seek out and face this painful situation again and again until we have mastered it, facing it with or without fear or hesitation, facing it until it ceases to be a "big deal." A deep satisfaction comes with this kind of mastery, and the joy of being alive deepens all the more.

Recently, the Dalai Lama was speaking on the nature of equanimity and the natural joy inherent in the mind. After one of his talks, a young reporter approached him and asked the following question. "Sir, the invaders have attempted to destroy your culture. They have burned your temples, and slaughtered the monks that you had raised from boyhood to be priests in your temples. How, sir, do you remain so joyful?"

After pausing for a moment, the Dalai Lama replied, "It is true that they have destroyed or taken these things. Shall I give them my mind too?"[12] How often do most of us give our minds away, time and again, each and every day? It is inspiring to see that it is possible for a human being to never leave that inherent joy. Is the Dalai Lama in denial? No. If you look at his life, you will see that he works day and night to reduce the ongoing violence and cruelty in his native Tibet. It is another one of our cultural myths to believe that we need to be angry and vengeful in order to deal with violence and injustice. Once again, we are reminded that the mind would always appear in its joyful and peaceful natural state if it were not for the doubts, fears, anger, and other disturbances that color it on a regular basis.

Love and Compassion

An accepting, loving, and non-reactive way of being seems to reflect or open us to our deeper, more authentic selves. Not easily described as either an emotion or disposition, compassion appears as a quality of one's very presence. An individual's compassion is something others can "feel." It seems to radiate out and touch all those within its reach. Without judgment, it calmly embraces whoever or whatever it meets.

Recall the last time that you loved so deeply that your thoughts, words, and actions just flowed from you. You said or did something kind, not because you owed someone a favor, not because you felt guilty about something you had said or done in the past, not because you wanted someone to like you, but simply because love was there in the moment. There was no sense of wanting something back from the other. Your love was truly selfless. You had no sense of ego or of being a separate self in those moments. There were no thoughts about your own safety or happiness. Rather than being someone who was "in love," you were literally "being love." Love itself was manifest without cause or condition.

"Being in love with" is an experience that has a sense of individuality or ego-self as its foundation or base, being some "one" who has love for someone else. From this level of awareness, "I love you" really means "I need you." This love has conditions. It is an "I love you if." "I love you if you do A and B, but if I catch you doing C or D, watch out!"

This conditional love is, of course, not true love at all. Rather, it represents a need or an emotional state that depends on whether or not one's needs are fulfilled. True love is compassionate and unconditional. It is sovereign, self-defined, and self-contained. It knows nothing of need.

Passion and Inspiration

When our hearts are open and we allow ourselves to be quiet enough to listen to the more subtle dimensions of our being, we begin to feel directed or guided in our lives. We feel a deeper calling. We are intuitively drawn toward certain individuals, projects, and places, while being guided away from others.

This emerging focus in life is often accompanied by feelings of inspiration and enthusiasm that come together as a true passion for life, an unfolding authenticity regarding the opportunities that life provides, a passionate search for truth that uses the events of life to more deeply investigate the nature of our inner essence or soul. The root meanings of the words inspiration *(in-spiritus)* and enthusiasm *(en-theos)* help us to understand their deeper meaning in the present context—to live life in the felt awareness of spirit and God.

We often ask others, "What do you love to do?" The question itself often elicits a smile. We like how we feel when reflecting on that which we love. Answers to this question often include dancing, singing, swimming, writing poetry, meditating, climbing mountains, listening to music, ice skating, riding motorcycles, painting, and so on. The issue here is not the specific activity or form but, rather, the feeling itself, the passion that lies within.

We then ask a follow-up question. "How long has it been since you have engaged in what you love to do?" At this point, the eyes turn downward and the person, often sadly, replies something like, "Well, it's been twenty years." The smile is now gone as the person realizes how long it has been since they have allowed themselves to feel the passion and joy that comes with engaging whatever it is that they feel inspired to do.

At this point we will ask, "What is that about? What has kept you from doing what you love for so long?" The answers that often follow reveal the degree to which the ego-self avoids the formless and unpredictable passion that lies within each of us because of its fear that this passion will be all-consuming. The ego-self resists dissolving. It does not want to lose control.

It does not want to die. Typical responses to our questioning include, "I don't have enough time," "I don't have enough money," "I haven't had the energy," "I don't have my spouse's support," "I don't feel well enough," and so on. Mary refers to these responses collectively as the "not enough syndrome," a habitually expressed belief that there is simply not enough to support or sustain us, physically, emotionally, or spiritually. If we continue in this way, the habit deepens, and pretty soon we feel as though we ourselves are not enough.

We disempower ourselves in this way, and often end up in dysfunctional and exaggerated coping strategies, such as becoming co-dependent or being overtly "macho." These strategies represent our attempts to deal with life, to hold onto our imagined sense of control, and to keep from drowning in our own fear and self-created sense of vulnerability. We seem to create an irresolvable situation for ourselves. We are afraid to die because we haven't lived. We're afraid to live fully because we don't want to die.

An eloquent exposition on how to face and resolve such issues is offered by Treya Wilber. At the time that she wrote this description, Treya was in the late stages of cancer. Her life situation afforded her a special opportunity to investigate the deeper dimensions of her experience. She died a short time after writing these words. "I was thinking about the Carmelites' emphasis on passion and the Buddhists' parallel emphasis on equanimity. It suddenly occurred to me that our normal understanding of what passion means is loaded with the idea of clinging, of wanting something or someone, of fearing losing them, of possessiveness. But what if you had passion without all that stuff, passion without attachment, passion clean and pure? What would that be like? What would that mean? I thought of those moments in meditation when I've felt my heart open, a painfully wonderful sensation, a passionate feeling but without clinging to any content or person or thing. And the two words suddenly coupled in my mind and made a whole. Passionate equanimity—to be fully passionate about all aspects of life, about one's relationship with spirit, to care to the depth of one's being but with no trace of clinging or holding, that's what the phrase has come to mean to me. It feels full, rounded, complete, and challenging."[13] Here is a clear and beautiful example of how one individual came to see the harmony in that which lies behind or within what initially appears to be separate, distinct, and conflictual—seeing the inherent unity in apparent differences.

What, then, would it be like to truly integrate these six qualities, or, asked in another way, what would it be like to live our lives as a confident, fearless, peaceful, joyful, loving, and inspired human being, every moment of every day with everyone we meet no matter what happens? Quite a challenge, to say the least, but a worthy challenge of the highest kind.

RECOGNIZING THE CHANGELESS: AN EXERCISE ON AGING

In order to help others begin to recognize the nature of that which doesn't change in their own experience, we offer an exercise that guides each person through their own personal aging process. The aging process, when viewed as such, offers another opportunity to contact the changeless amidst the unrelenting changes in life.[14]

More specifically, each person is asked, in their mind's eye, to go back in time. They are first asked to go back to when they were four years old. They are asked to see themselves at the age of four, both physically—"What do you look like?"—and in terms of their feelings—"How do you feel?" After a minute or so, they are asked to see themselves slowly aging until they reach the age of ten, seeing themselves at the age of ten, and answering the same questions as before. "What do you look like?" and "How do you feel?" This same process of visualization and questioning continues for the ages eighteen, thirty, forty-five, sixty, seventy-five, and ninety years of age.

Following this sequence, individuals are then guided back to their present age at which point they are asked two basic questions regarding the process that they have just completed. The first question is, "As you experienced yourself aging from four years old through your teens and mid-life to being 90 years old, what changed during this time?" Answers to this question usually come fairly quickly and often include, "my body," "my moods," "my opinions," "my hopes," "my likes and dislikes," and "the pleasures and pains of life."

Following a period of discussion, the second question is then asked. "During this lifelong process of growing older, what doesn't change?" Unlike the first question, where answers come to mind quite easily, a noticeable silence usually follows this second question. During this silence, we often reword the question. "As you age from four years old through ten, eighteen, thirty, forty-five, sixty, seventy-five, and ninety years of age, what remains the same—untainted, unaltered, impermeable, and untouched by all the changes that occur in life?" Eventually, someone will say something like, "Well, it's always 'me' no matter what age I am or what has happened in my life. The sense of 'I' or 'I am' is always there."

Encouraging the person to investigate their response more deeply, we then ask, "Yes, that seems true, but what lies behind or beneath the concept or thought of 'me,' 'I,' or 'I am'? What is the experience or felt sense behind this concept or thought?" Again, there is usually silence as the person begins to see that this deeper, more subtle feeling is somehow one with the silence. It lies within or merged with absolute stillness itself—a silent state of being —pure consciousness, pure awareness, without the slightest movement or disturbance.

The moment that a thought or question appears, such as—"What is this?" or "What does 'I am' really mean?"—the silence is broken, the stillness is gone, and the person has stepped out of the foundational peace back into his or her reflecting, thinking, reactive mind. A discussion again follows where hopefully each individual will experience, or at least taste (some for the very first time), the peace and quiet that lies deep within them, the silence that is always there, perhaps touching that thread that runs, unaffected and unchanged, through one's entire life.

THE NATURE OF PAIN AND SUFFERING

If our nature is to be confident, fearless, peaceful, joyful, loving, and inspired, then what is all this suffering? A great yogi and spiritual teacher of India, Ramana Maharshi, while dying of cancer, was heard crying out in pain late one evening by one of his disciples. His disciple was puzzled by this since his master had repeatedly demonstrated his healing powers and control over his own bodily functions throughout his life. How could the master be suffering? When approached by his disciple, Ramana Maharshi said, "Yes, I am experiencing pain, but I am not suffering." It seems that he was so deeply connected with his eternal, unchanging nature that the pain of his cancer did not disturb this Self-identification.

What does it mean to experience intense pain, but not to suffer? For most everyone, pain and suffering are inseparably one and the same. Ancient and modern wisdom alike tell us that we suffer because we are attached to how we think life should be. We are simply not content with the way life is, repeatedly basing our happiness on whether things turn out the way we want and/or need them to be. This is a conditional happiness dependent on the unpredictable and ever-changing world, rather than an authentic happiness rooted in the pure joy and changeless reality that lies within.

The *Hsin Hsin Ming,* attributed to Sengtsan, the Third Zen Patriarch, begins, "The Great Way is simple for those who have no preferences. Make the slightest distinction, however, and heaven and earth are set infinitely apart."[15] These words do not just refer to our more mundane, day-to-day preferences: Do you prefer the taste of chocolate to vanilla? or Do you like Toyotas more than Chevrolets? Rather, they raise more profound questions. Do you prefer life over death? Do you prefer pleasure over pain? In response to these questions, most of us have an egocentric voice inside that says, "You bet!"

What is being suggested here, however, is that, until that part of you that has a preference becomes quiet and nonreactive, it is not going to be easy. When you have grief, can you turn towards it, feel it, express it, and not run the other way? It feels counter-instinctive, at least at first, to turn and face the pain, but that is what the ancient wisdom suggests.

If you want to find that great treasure within, you cannot jump over these painful levels. You must go through them, not because you like pain or that you are masochistic on some level, but because it is real. If you feel like crying, then cry. If someone else is uncomfortable with your tears, that discomfort reflects their resistance to feeling their own unacknowledged and unexpressed pain. When someone is sobbing in grief, how often do we hear statements like, "You've got to get over it!" or "You've got to stop crying and get on with your life." What such people are really saying is, "I'm uncomfortable in your presence when you're expressing your grief because I don't want to feel my own. Please stop."

The implication here is that if you do hold these preferences for pleasure and life, then you will suffer since pain is part of life, and death is inevitable. Have you ever noticed that when you are happy and "on top of the world," you can't imagine ever being depressed again, and when you are deeply depressed and all seems dark and hopeless, you can't remember or even imagine what it was like to be happy and content? At these times, heaven and earth are truly set infinitely apart.

Stephen Levine, in an early 1990 lecture he gave in San Francisco, raised another important issue regarding the mind and attachment. He said that, "Everyone thinks that the issues related to our basic drives—hunger, thirst, sleep, sex, and survival—reflect our deepest attachments." Everyone sitting in the audience nodded in agreement at this point. Stephen continued, "These attachments, however, are nothing compared to our deepest attachment of all, our attachment to pain!"[16]

Now his audience was puzzled. What could he possibly mean? Pain is something to avoid, not something to hold onto. Stephen purposely offered a simple example to both illustrate his point, and to remind us that aversion, as well as attraction, can be a breeding ground for attachment. "Imagine you have decided to hang a picture and you are in the process of using a hammer to pound a nail in the wall. But then, in the process of nailing, you accidentally miss the nail and hit your thumb with the hammer. What is usually your first response when things like this occur? Many of us swear at this point ('Damn!') or begin a series of self-condemning thoughts ('You idiot. You clumsy jerk! You can't do the simplest thing without screwing up!') Isn't it interesting that, at a time when your body needs love, kindness, and soothing thoughts the most, you send judgment, negativity, and greater pain?" The mind's inclination to react with painful thoughts, though seemingly counter-instinctive, runs very deep. For most of us, this habit of mind that contracts around and holds onto pain in this way is very difficult to change.

From this perspective, the root cause of suffering lies in our own minds. Hari Dass emphasized this point when he said, "Until you realize at the core of your being that you have created and are, therefore, responsible for every last content of your mind, true spiritual realization cannot even begin."[17] What he is implying here is that if you continue to blame outside events in general, and others in particular, for your unhappiness ("He made me angry." "She made me jealous." "I am depressed because I lost my job.") then one cannot begin to comprehend the deeper spiritual truths that require an unwavering identification with the sovereign spiritual Self—with that which remains unchanged, unaffected by the opinions of others and the events of the world.

Swami Veda once commented that blaming another person for your feelings is a spiritual insanity plea.[18] He is not saying that blaming another is pathological in the everyday world. In fact, this habit is accepted, even encouraged, and seen as quite normal. But, rather, if realizing your true, sovereign, spiritual nature or Self is really what you are after, then giving your power away to the words and actions of another is "crazy."

This also holds true when you attribute the cause of your happiness to someone or something outside yourself. "I can only be happy with you my love!," "I'm so happy because it didn't rain today." You are again forgetting your sacred nature, the pure, clear, unchanging Self that is beyond both pleasure and pain.

Ramana Maharshi did not suffer because his inner spiritual identity was solid. He was not attached to comfort. The Buddha taught that we need only to stop clinging to things of this world in order to end our suffering. In the Judeo-Christian tradition, letting go of attachment is explicitly implied in "surrendering to the Will of God." The Bhagavad Gita advises us to not be attached to the fruits of our actions. Carlos Castaneda describes the "man of knowledge" as an "impeccable warrior."[19] An impeccable warrior is one who thinks, speaks, and acts solely from his or her quiet, intuitive center and proceeds to carry out, with full concentration and energy, all that is deemed necessary in order to serve this vision without the slightest concern for the outcome of these efforts and actions. Here is yet another example of the individual who lives in the world but not of it.

Pain is a natural part of life. To avoid pain by seeking comfort often entails control and manipulation. Outcomes are of more than great importance when control and manipulation are center stage. They are essential. In stark contrast, living the sacred life is largely a matter of acceptance. As Joseph Sharp has said, "One is a matter of holding on and aligning with our egoic wants and desires; the other is surrender, opening, and letting go."[20]

Death opens the door to the treasure that lies within. We cannot jump over the pains of life into the eternal peace and joy that characterize this treasure. We can, however, live our lives with awareness, open to and integrate our life experiences, and, thereby, come to realize the other side. Opening to dying and grieving are optimal ways to reach this end. The grief that follows the death of a loved one shatters the mind's habitual patterns.

Ego death takes us to the world beyond attachment. Physical death takes us to the realm beyond form.

> All praise be yours, my Lord, for Sister death,
> From whose embrace no mortal can escape ...
> Happy for those She finds doing your Will!
> For the second death can do no harm to them.
>
> Francis of Assisi
> *A Prayer for Every Weather*

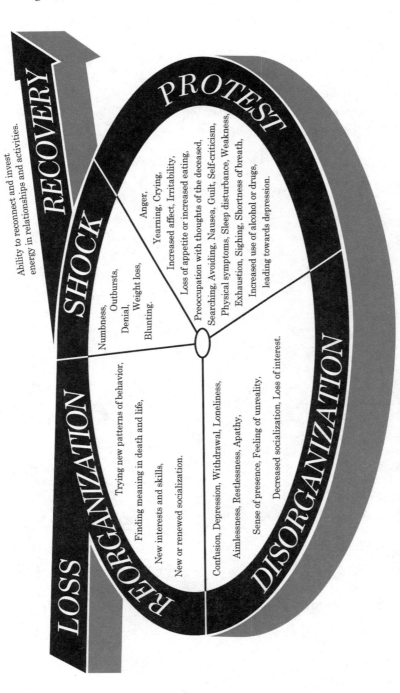

Figure 1. Adapted from a model by William M. Lamers, M.D.

Figure 2

THE GRIEF EXPERIENCE

Mary Mohs, L.V.N., M.A.

As one grieves, one goes through a variety of experiences on different levels: physical, behavioral, cognitive, emotional, and spiritual.

Physically, a person may experience:
1. a tightness in the throat or chest
2. a sensitivity to noise
3. a sense of depersonalization; nothing seems real
4. shortness of breath
5. dry mouth
6. a lack of energy
7. muscles feeling weak
8. a hollowness in the stomach and/or stomach pain
9. heart palpitations
10. an increase in blood pressure

Behaviorally, a person may experience:
1. sleep and appetite disturbances
2. absent mindedness due to a preoccupation with the loss
3. withdrawal
4. dreams about the person who died
5. putting all pictures of the loved-one away
6. avoiding visiting places where the deceased had been in order to avoid remembering (often due to an ambivalent relationship)
7. searching for the loved-one, and calling out to him or her
8. sighing, restlessness, crying, overactivity
9. visiting places the loved-one used to frequent
10. carrying objects that remind him or her of the loved-one
11. wearing the clothes and treasuring objects that belonged to the person who died

Cognitively, a person may experience:
1. disbelief—it takes a long time to grasp the loss on all levels
2. preoccupation—thinking about the person who died almost constantly at first
3. a sense of the loved-one's presence, with or without visual and/or auditory "hallucinations"
4. thought patterns having to do with sadness and depression (e.g., "I can't live without her," "It was my fault he died.") It is common for one to say, "I don't want to live."

Emotionally, a person may experience:
1. sadness—missing the person who died
2. anger (often with confusion). "He didn't plan to die," rage-displacement
3. guilt, self-reproach, not being able to do enough for the person (usually around the date/time of his/her death)
4. anxiety—usually from two sources: fear of not being able to do without the loved one, and a heightened sense of death (one's own and in general)
5. loneliness—missing the person who died, especially if one lived with him or her
6. shock—more often occurs with sudden death
7. yearning—wanting the loved-one back
8. relief—usually when the person dies following a long illness

Spiritually, a person may experience:
1. his or her identity shifting—feelings of emptiness, void, denseness
2. feeling held or protected; one may notice synchronicities
3. feeling betrayed by and/or angry at God and others (one may decide there is no God)
4. going on a quest to find out where the loved-one has gone, who God is, and what is the meaning of life
5. a deeper personal awareness
6. his or her inner experience becoming more important

7. feeling joy, noticing nature more, and being more in tune with life (even while going through the pain of the loss)
8. relationships becoming more important
9. material possessions feeling less important
10. becoming more service-oriented

The first four categories are revised from Worden, J. William. *Grief Counseling and Grief Therapy: A Handbook for the Mental Health Practitioner.* New York: Springer, 1982.

Figure 3

DISTINCTIONS BETWEEN DEPRESSIVE GRIEF AND CLINICAL DEPRESSION

DEPRESSIVE GRIEF	CLINICAL DEPRESSION
Responds to comfort and support	Does not accept support
Often openly angry	Irritable and may complain, but does not directly express anger
Relates depressed feelings to loss experienced	Does not relate experiences to a particular life event
Can still experience moments of enjoyment in life	Exhibits an all-pervading sense of doom
Exhibits feelings of sadness and emptiness	Projects a sense of hopelessness and chronic emptiness
May have transient physical complaints	Has chronic physical complaints
Expresses guilt over some specific aspect of the loss	Has generalized feelings of guilt
Has temporary impact upon self-esteem	Loss of self-esteem is of greater duration

From Wolfelt, Alan. *Death and Grief: A Guide for Clergy.* Muncie, IN: Accelerated Development Publishers, 1988.

Notes

PREFACE

1. Please note that small changes in the original draft of this Preface were made by the authors for the sake of stylistic consistency and clarity, especially for those unfamiliar with the Himalayan Yoga tradition.
2. See Swami Veda Bharati's *Mahabharata: Bhishma*. Rishikesh, India: SRSG Publications, 2004.
3. The text *Sanatsujatiya,* a part of the *Mahabharata*, has been translated by Swami Veda Bharati as part of the *Companion Texts to the Bhagavad-Gita,* a planned and incomplete series. Photocopies are available by request.
4. The three epithets of *atman* (soul) repeated emphatically throughout the Vedic texts.
5. See *Yoga-Sutras of Patanjali* 1.9, Swami Veda Bharati's Commentary. The stock example of a *vikalpa* is given in the texts as:

> Here goes the son of a barren woman.
> He has worn a crown of sky-flowers.
> Having bathed in the waters of a mirage,
> He carries a bow made of hare's horns.

INTRODUCTION

1. Ardagh, Arjuna. "Cultivating Translucence: A Curriculum for a Saner Planet," *Shift: At The Frontiers of Consciousness,* 8 (2005): 28-32, 29.

CHAPTER 1: LIVING, DYING, AND GRIEVING

1. For a detailed and personal commentary on the life and teachings of Swami Rama see O'Brien, Justin (Swami Jaidev Bharati). *Walking with a Himalayan Master: An American's Odyssey*. St. Paul: Yes International Publishers, 2005.
2. King, Theresa. "What Is Spirituality?" In *The Spiral Path: Explorations in Women's Spirituality,* edited by Theresa King. St. Paul: Yes International Publishers, 1992, 13.
3. See, for example, Leech, Peter and Singer, Zeva. *Acknowledgment: Opening to the Grief of Unacceptable Loss.* Laytonville, CA: Wintercreek, 1988; Staudacher, Carol. *Beyond Grief: A Guide for Recovering from the Death of a Loved One.* Oakland, CA: New Harbinger, 1987; Tatelbaum, Judy. *The Courage to Grieve: Creative Living, Recovery, and Growth through Grief.* New York: Harper & Row, 1980.
4. See Peck, M. Scott. *Denial of the Soul: Spiritual and Medical Perspectives on Euthanasia and Mortality.* New York: Harmony Books, 1997.
5. DuBois, Paul. *The Hospice Way of Death.* New York: Human Sciences Press, 1980.
6. Kubler-Ross, Elisabeth. *On Death and Dying.* New York: Macmillan, 1969; *Living*

with Death and Dying. New York: Macmillan, 1981; *The Wheel of Life: A Memoir of Living and Dying.* New York: Scribner, 1997; *The Tunnel and the Light: Essential Insights on Living and Dying.* New York: Marlowe & Company, 1999; Kubler-Ross, Elisabeth and Kessler, David. *Life Lessons.* New York: Scribner, 2000.

7. For example, Kessler, David. *The Needs of the Dying: A Guide for Bringing Hope, Comfort, and Love to Life's Final Chapter.* New York: Perennial Currents, 2000.

8. Moody, Raymond. *Life after Life.* New York: Bantam Books, 1975; *Reflections on Life after Life.* New York: Bantam Books, 1977.

9. See also Bailey, Lee Worth and Yates, Jenny, editors. *The Near-Death Experience: A Reader.* New York: Routledge, 1996; Morse, Melvin and Perry, Paul. *Transformed by the Light: The Powerful Effect of Near-Death Experiences on People's Lives.* New York: Villard Books, 1992; Ring, Kenneth. *Heading toward Omega: In Search of the Meaning of the Near-Death Experience.* New York: William Morrow, 1984.

10. Ram Dass. *Remember: Be Here Now.* Albuquerque: Lama Foundation, 1971; *Still Here: Embracing Aging, Changing, and Dying.* New York: Riverhead Books, 2000.

11. Levine, Stephen. *Who Dies? An Investigation of Conscious Living and Conscious Dying.* Garden City: Anchor Press, 1982; *Meetings at the Edge: Dialogues with the Grieving and the Dying, the Healing and the Healed.* Garden City: Anchor Press, 1984; *Healing into Life and Death.* Garden City: Anchor Press, 1987.

12. See Tieger, Joseph and Luther, Johanna, producers. *How Then Shall We Live?* video series. Oakland: Original Face Video, 1987. For writings consistent with this perspective, see The Dalai Lama. *The Joy of Living and Dying in Peace.* San Francisco: Harper San Francisco, 1997; and Singh, Kathleen Dowling. *The Grace in Dying: How We Are Transformed Spiritually As We Die.* San Francisco: Harper San Francisco, 1998.

13. Ram Dass and Gorman, Paul. *How Can I Help? Stories and Reflections on Service.* New York: Alfred A. Knopf, 1985.

14. Adapted from Borglum, Dale. Brochure. Novato, CA: Living/Dying Project, 1991.

15. Rama, Swami. *Sacred Journey: Living Purposefully and Dying Gracefully.* New Delhi: Himalayan International Institute of Yoga Science and Philosophy, 1996.

16. Tigunait, Rajmani. *From Death to Birth: Understanding Karma and Reincarnation.* Honesdale, PA: Himalayan Institute Press, 1997.

17. From Valle, Ron, "Reflections of a Volunteer," In *Living/Dying Project Newsletter,* September, 1988, 1.

CHAPTER 2: THE PROCESS OF DYING

1. Tyndale, William, translator. *The Living Bible.* Wheaton, IL: Tyndale House Publishers, 1982.

2. Kubler-Ross, Elisabeth. *On Death and Dying.* New York: Macmillan, 1969.

3. Levine, Stephen. *Who Dies? An Investigation of Conscious Living and Conscious Dying.* Garden City: Anchor Press, 1982.

4. *Ibid.,* 239.

5. *Ibid.,* 239.

6. Tyndale, *op.cit.*

7. See Levine, *op.cit.,* 243-246.

CHAPTER 3: ON BEING WITH DYING

1. Longaker, Christine. *Facing Death and Finding Hope: A Guide to the Emotional and Spiritual Care of the Dying.* New York: Doubleday, 1997.

2. von Franz, Marie-Louise. *Dreams: A Study of the Dreams of Jung, Descartes, Socrates, and Other Historical Figures.* Boston: Shambhala, 1998.

3. Levine, Stephen. *Who Dies? An Investigation of Conscious Living and Conscious Dying.* Garden City: Anchor Press, 1982, 73-74.

4. Rinpoche, Sogyal. *The Tibetan Book of Living and Dying.* San Francisco: Harper San Francisco, 1992, 219.

5. Tyndale, William, translator. *The Living Bible.* Wheaton, IL: Tyndale House Publishers, 1982.

6. *Ibid.*

7. See, for example, Ram Dass. *Paths to God: Living the Bhagavad Gita.* New York: Harmony Books, 2004; Rama, Swami. *Perennial Psychology of the Bhagavad Gita.* Honesdale, PA: Himalayan Press, 1985; Yogananda, Paramahansa. *The Bhagavad Gita: Royal Science of God-Realization.* Chapters 1-5. Los Angeles: Self-Realization Fellowship, 1995.

8. For a comparison of Christianity and Yoga as spiritual traditions, see O'Brien, Justin. *A Meeting of Mystic Paths: Christianity and Yoga.* Saint Paul: Yes International Publishers, 1996.

9. Sharp, Joseph. *Living Our Dying: A Way to the Sacred in Everyday Life.* New York: Hyperion, 1996, 116.

CHAPTER 4: GRIEF AND THE GRIEVING PROCESS

1. For example, Archer, John. *The Nature of Grief: The Evolution and Psychology of Reactions to Loss.* New York: Routledge, 1999; Bowlby, John. *Loss: Sadness and Depression.* New York: Basic Books, 1980; Brown-Saltzman, Katherine. "Transforming the Grief Process." In Carroll-Johnson, Rose Mary and Bush, Nancy Jo, editors. *Psychosocial Nursing Care: Along the Cancer Continuum.* Pittsburgh: Oncology Nursing Press, 1998; Corless, Inge. "Bereavement." In Ferrell, Betty and Coyle, Nessa, editors. *Textbook of Palliative Nursing Care.* New York: Oxford University Press, 2001; Doka, Kenneth. "Grief." In Kastenbaum, Robert and Kastenbaum, Beatrice, editors. *Encyclopedia of Death.* Phoenix: Oryx Press, 1989; Kessler, David and Kubler-Ross, Elisabeth. *On Grief and Grieving: Finding the Meaning of Grief through the Five Stages of Loss.* New York: Scribner, 2005; Lindemann, Erich. "Symptomology and Management of Acute Grief," *American Journal of Psychiatry.* Sesquicentennial Supplement, 151(6), 1994, 155-160; Parkes, Colin Murray. *Bereavement: Studies of Grief in Adult Life.* Madison, CT: International Universities Press, 1998; Rando, Therese. *Treatment of Complicated Mourning.* Champaign: Research Press, 1993; Sanders, Catherine. *Surviving Grief and Learning to Live Again.* New York: John Wiley, 1992; Worden, J. William. *Grief Counseling and Grief Therapy: A Handbook for the Mental Health Practitioner.* New York: Springer, 1991.

2. Kubler-Ross, Elisabeth. *On Death and Dying.* New York: Macmillan, 1969.

3. See Conner, Mary. "Understanding the Cycle of Normal Grief in Adult Patients,"

University of Minnesota, Department of Family Practice and Community Health, *Behavioral Medicine Briefs*. March, 1999, 1-2; Lamers, Jr., William M. "On the Psychology of Loss." In Bertman, Sandra, editor. *Grief and the Healing Arts: Creativity as Therapy. Death, Value, and Meaning*. Amityville, NY: Baywood Publishing Company, 1999, 21-38.

4. Levine, Stephen. *Meetings at the Edge: Dialogues with the Grieving and the Dying, the Healing and the Healed*. Garden City: Anchor Press, 1984, 31.

5. Levine, Stephen. *Who Dies? An Investigation of Conscious Living and Conscious Dying*. Garden City: Anchor Press, 1982, 189.

6. Jung, Carl. *Memories, Dreams, Reflections*. New York: Vintage Books, 1989.

7. de Mello, Anthony. *The Way to Love: The Last Meditations of Anthony de Mello*. New York: Doubleday, 1992, 134.

8. Kubler-Ross, Elisabeth. *Death: The Final Stage of Growth*. Englewood Cliffs: Prentice-Hall, 1975.

9. Rando, *op.cit.*, 209.

10. Blum, Joanne. "Food for New Thought: Spiritual Gifts of Depression," *Unity Magazine*, April, 1996.

11. Rosen, David. *Transforming Depression: A Jungian Approach Using the Creative Arts*. New York: Putnam, 1993, 3.

12. *Ibid.*, 4.

13. Levine, 1982, *op.cit.*

14. *Ibid.*, 241.

15. See Nancee Sobonya's presentation on the "gifts of grief." Sobonya, Nancee, producer. *The Gifts of Grief*, video. Oakland, CA: Shining Light Productions, 2005.

16. Levine, 1982, *op.cit.*, 234.

17. Levine, 1984, *op.cit.*, 105.

18. For example, Romanyshyn, Robert. *The Soul in Grief: Love, Death, and Transformation*. Berkeley: North Atlantic Books, 1999; Gayton, Richard. *The Forgiving Place: Choosing Peace after Violent Trauma*. Waco, TX: WRS Publishing, 1995; and Welshons, John. *Awakening From Grief: Finding the Way Back to Joy*. Makawao, Maui: Inner Ocean Publishing, 2003.

19. Levine, 1984 *op.cit.*, 31.

20. Hume, Robert Ernest, translator. *The Thirteen Principal Upanishads*. New York: Oxford University Press, 1971, 353.

21. Tyndale, William, translator. *The Living Bible*. Wheaton, IL: Tyndale House Publishers, 1982.

22. Rama, Swami. *Sacred Journey: Living Purposefully and Dying Gracefully*. New Delhi: Himalayan International Institute of Yoga Science and Philosophy, 1996, 25.

23. Tyndale, *op.cit.*

CHAPTER 5: THE PASSAGE THROUGH GRIEF

1. Mohs, Mary. "Grief: A Road to Transcendence," *Rose Street Center Newsletter*, 1(2), 1992, 3.

2. Jung, Carl. *Memories, Dreams, Reflections*. New York: Vintage Books, 1989.

3. Johnson, Robert. *Inner Work*. San Francisco: Harper & Row, 1986.

4. Radha, Swami. *Realities of the Dreaming Mind*. Spokane: Timeless Books, 1994.

5. Rama, Swami. *Sacred Journey: Living Purposefully and Dying Gracefully*. New Delhi: Himalayan International Institute of Yoga Science and Philosophy, 1996.

6. For a detailed overview of the physiology and benefits of diaphragmatic breathing, see Nuernberger, Phil. *Freedom from Stress: A Holistic Approach*. Honesdale, PA: Himalayan Institute Press, 1981; and Rama, Swami, Ballentine, Rudolph, and Hymes, Alan. *Science of Breath: A Practical Guide*. Honesdale, PA: Himalayan Institute Press, 1979.

7. O'Brien, Justin. *The Wellness Tree*. Saint Paul: Yes International Publishers, 1993, 6.

8. Levine, Stephen. *Who Dies? An Investigation of Conscious Living and Conscious Dying*. Garden City: Anchor Press, 1982, 220-225.

9. For example, Almaas, A.H. *The Pearl Beyond Price; Integration of Personality into Being: An Object Relations Approach*. Berkeley: Diamond Books, 1988.

10. Welwood, John. *Journey of the Heart*. New York: Harper Collins, 1990, 144.

11. Tyndale, William, translator. *The Living Bible*. Wheaton, IL: Tyndale House Publishers, 1982.

12. Tolle, Eckhart. *The Power of Now: A Guide to Spiritual Enlightenment*. Novato, CA: New World Library, 1999, 75.

13. Keating, Thomas. *Open Mind, Open Heart*. New York: Continuum Publishing Company, 1992, 138.

14. In Ward, Tom. "Centering Prayer: An Overview." In *Sewanee Theological Review*, 40(1), 1996, 18-28.

15. Tigunait, Rajmani. *Why We Fight: Practices for Lasting Peace*. Honesdale, PA: Himalayan Institute Press, 2003, 10.

16. See, for example, Arya, Usharbudh. *Superconcious Meditation*. Honesdale, PA: Himalayan Press, 1978; Johnsen, Linda. *Meditation Is Boring: Putting Life in Your Spiritual Practice*. Honesdale, PA: Himalayan Institute Press, 2000.

17. From Valle, Ron. "The Emergence of Transpersonal Psychology." In Valle, Ron and Halling, Steen, editors. *Existential-Phenomenological Perspectives in Psychology: Exploring the Breadth of Human Experience*. New York: Plenum Press, 1989, 257-268.

18. Arya, Usharbudh. *Meditation and the Art of Dying*. Honesdale, PA: Himalayan Press, 1979.

CHAPTER 6: MOVING TOWARD THE SACRED

1. David-Neel, Alexandra. *Buddhism: Its Doctrines and Its Methods*. New York: Avon Books, 1977; Nhat Hanh, Thich. *No Death, No Fear: Comforting Wisdom for Life*. New York: Riverhead Books, 2002.

2. Veda Bharati, Swami. Personal communication, 1993.

3. Grof, Christina. *The Thirst for Wholeness: Attachment, Addiction, and the Spiritual Path*. San Francisco: Harper Collins, 1994, 154.

4. Rama, Swami. *Sacred Journey: Living Purposefully and Dying Gracefully*. New Delhi: Himalayan International Institute of Yoga Science and Philosophy, 1996, 1.

5. For a further discussion regarding attachment, addiction, and the fear of death, see

Mohs, Mary, Valle, Ron, and Butko, Audrey. *Transpersonal Perspectives in the Nature and Treatment of Substance Abuse.* Brentwood, CA: Awakening Press, 1997.

6. Tolle, Eckhart. *The Power of Now: A Guide to Spiritual Enlightenment.* Novato, CA: New World Library, 1999, 56.

7. Tyndale, William, translator. *The Living Bible.* Wheaton: Tyndale House Publishers, 1982.

8. Ram Dass, from "An Evening with Ram Dass" in Pittsburgh, April, 1979.

9. Huxley, Aldous. *The Perennial Philosophy.* New York: Harper & Row, 1970.

10. Swing, William. Personal communication, 1999.

11. Nuernberger, Phil. "Overcoming Fear." In *Yoga International,* 4(3), 1994, 21-27.

12. The Dalai Lama from his "Living in Peace" lecture in Berkeley, CA, May 2002.

13. In Wilber, Ken. *Grace and Grit: Spirituality and Healing in the Life and Death of Treya Killam Wilber.* Boston: Shambhala, 1991, 338-339.

14. Valle, Ron and Mohs, Mary. "Aging with Awareness." In Schlitz, Marilyn, Amorok, Tina, and Micozzi, Marc, editors. *Consciousness and Healing: Integral Approaches to Mind-Body Medicine.* St.Louis: Elsevier, 2004, 193-201.

15. Sengtsan. *Hsin Hsin Ming: Verses on the Faith-Mind.* Toronto: The Coach House Press, 1973, 1.

16. Stephen Levine from his presentation with Ondrea Levine, "Conscious Living/Conscious Dying" in San Francisco, April, 1990.

17. Hari Dass. Personal communication, 1985.

18. Veda Bharati, Swami. Personal communication, 1983.

19. Castaneda, Carlos. *The Teachings of Don Juan: A Yaqui Way of Knowledge.* New York: Ballentine Books, 1968; *A Separate Reality: Further Conversations with Don Juan.* New York: Simon and Schuster, 1971.

20. Sharp, Joseph. *Living Our Dying: A Way to the Sacred in Everyday Life.* New York: Hyperion, 1996, 119.

About the Authors

Ron Valle, Ph.D. has served as a psychologist for over twenty years. He specializes in helping clients with chronic pain and stress-related disorders and with individuals and families who face a life-threatening diagnosis. A long-time practitioner and teacher of meditation, Ron developed the Integrated Therapy Program for Transforming Stress and Pain while director of an outpatient university hospital pain clinic. Professor, supervisor, counselor, minister, and author of a wide variety of professional publications, he currently serves as a director of Awakening: A Center for Exploring Living and Dying, as well as the Awakening Retreat Center in Brentwood, California. He is also the editor of *Phenomenological Inquiry: Existential and Transpersonal Dimensions* and senior editor of *Metaphors of Consciousness*.

Mary Mohs, L.V.N., M.A., M.A.C. has her master's degree in Transpersonal Counseling Psychology. Her life's work has included working with the dying and grieving for over twenty years as well as being a nurse and certified substance abuse counselor. Her extensive study of both eastern and western spiritual philosophies and approaches to life has deepened her understanding of her own spirituality and reflects her interest in the commonalities among all of the world's religions. Mary serves as a director of Awakening: A Center for Exploring Living and Dying as well as the Awakening Retreat Center in Brentwood, California. She has written and published a number of articles and chapters addressing living, dying, and grieving, and has taught courses on these and other subjects from a transpersonal perspective at the graduate level.

Awakening: A Center for Exploring Living and Dying is a nonprofit educational and service organization whose purpose is to offer encouragement and support to those who seek the direct personal experience of the sacred within. As a community, we see every aspect of living and dying as an opportunity to deepen one's compassion, self-understanding, and spiritual awareness, especially situations that involve a life-threatening diagnosis, coping with the effects of a serious accident or illness, or grieving the death of a loved one.

The Awakening Retreat Center is an interfaith center designed to provide a supportive environment for individuals and groups exploring ways to integrate their work in the world with their spiritual lives. Located in the foothills of Mt. Diablo in Brentwood, California, the center provides a beautiful and peaceful setting for personal and group retreats. www.awakeningonline.com.

Yes International Publishers

Publishers of award-winning Books, CDs and DVDs
on spirituality, yoga, wellness, self-transformation, and inspiration.

Books on Spiritual Growth, Mysticism, and Yoga:

Walking with a Himalayan Master: An American's Odyssey
Justin O'Brien, Ph.D. (Swami Jaidev Bharati)

A Meeting of Mystic Paths: Christianity and Yoga
Justin O'Brien, Ph.D.

The Laughing Swami
Edited by Swami Jaidev and Ma Devi

Three Paths of Devotion
Prem Prakash

The Spiral Path: Explorations into Women's Spirituality
Theresa King

The Divine Mosaic: Women's Images of the Sacred Other
Theresa King

The Yogi: Portraits of Swami Vishnu-devananda
Gopala Krishna

The Living Goddess: Reclaiming the Mother of the Universe
Linda Johnsen

Daughters of the Goddess: The Women Saints of India
Linda Johnsen

Streams from the Sacred River: Women's Spiritual Wisdom
Mary Pinney Erickson & Betty Kling

Subtler than the Subtle: The Upanishad of the White Horse
Swami Veda Bharati

Circle of Mysteries: A Women's Rosary Book
Christin Lore Weber

The Warrior Sage
Phil Nuernberger, Ph.D.

The Art of Superconscious Meditation
Swami Jaidev Bharati

Books on Health and Personal Growth:

The Wellness Tree: Six-step Program for Creating Optimal Wellness
    Justin O'Brien, Ph.D.
Running and Breathing
    Justin O'Brien, Ph.D.
A Thousand Suns: Designing Your Future with Vedic Astrology
    Linda Johnsen
Strong and Fearless: The Quest for Personal Power
    Phil Nuernberger, Ph.D
Ransoming the Mind: An Integration of Yoga and Modern Therapy
    Charles Bates
Pigs Eat Wolves: Going into Partnership with your Dark Side
    Charles Bates
Mirrors: Affirmations & Actions for Daily Reflection
    Cheryl Wall
Mirrors for Men: Affirmations & Actions for Daily Reflection
    Justin O'Brien
Opening to Dying and Grieving: A Sacred Journey
    Ron Valle and Mary Mohs

Inspirational Poetry:

Soulfire: Love Poems in Black and Gold
    Alla Renée Bozarth
The Light of Ten Thousand Suns
    Swami Veda Bharati

Journal:

Himalayan Path
    A quarterly publication of the Himalayan Tradition of Yoga

For more information, a catalog, or to order:

Yes International Publishers
1317 Summit Avenue
Saint Paul, MN 55105-2602
651-645-6808 • 800-431-1579
www.yespublishers.com